GODS
IN OUR MIDST

GODS
IN OUR MIDST

Mythological Images
of the Masculine:
A Woman's View

Christine Downing

CROSSROAD · NEW YORK

1993

The Crossroad Publishing Company
370 Lexington Avenue, New York, NY 10017

Printed in the United States of America

Library of Congress Cataloging-in-Publication Data

Downing, Christine, 1931–
    Gods in our midst : mythological images of the masculine : a
woman's view / Christine Downing.
        p. cm.
    Includes bibliographical references and index.
    ISBN 0-8245-1242-1 (hard)
    1. Women–Religious life. 2.Gods, Greek–Psychological aspects.
3. Mythology, Greek–Psychological aspects. 4. Masculinity
(Psychology) 5. Archetype (Psychology) 6. Women–Psychology.
I. Title.
BL625.7.D68 1993
292.2'113–dc20   92-40146
                                                                          CIP

Grateful acknowledgment is made to the following persons and publishers for permission to quote from published material:

Macmillan Publishing Company: for 8 lines from "Leda and the Swan," from *Collected Poems* by W. B. Yeats. Copyright 1928 by Macmillan Publishing Company, renewed 1956 by Georgie Yeats. Reprinted by permission of Macmillan Publishing Company.

New Directions: for various lines from the following poems by H.D.: "The Islands," "Hermes of the Ways," "The God," "Evadne," "At Piraeus," "Delphi," and "Dodona," from *Collected Poems 1912-1944* by H.D. Copyright © 1928 by the Estate of Hilda Doolittle. Reprinted by permission of New Directions Publishing Corporation.

W. W. Norton & Company, Inc.: for 11 lines from "At Delphi," from *Collected Poems (1930-1973)* by May Sarton. Copyright © 1974 by May Sarton. Reprinted by permission of W. W. Norton & Company, Inc.

Random House, Inc.: for 3 lines from "Orpheus. Eurydice. Hermes," from *The Selected Poetry of Rainer Maria Rilke,* translated by Stephen Mitchell. Copyright © 1982 by Stephen Mitchell. Reprinted by permission of Random House, Inc.

Spring Publications: 14 lines from "The Hymn to Hermes," from *The Homeric Hymns,* translated by Charles Boer. 2d revised edition. Dallas: Spring Publications, 1979. Reprinted by permission of Spring Publications.

The University of Chicago Press: for 3 lines from *The Iliad of Homer,* translated by Richmond Lattimore. The University of Chicago Press, 1951. Reprinted by permission of The University of Chicago Press.

Vintage Books: 11 lines from *The Odyssey of Homer,* translated by R. Fitzgerald. Copyright© 1962, 1963 by Robert Fitzgerald and renewed 1989 by Benedict R. C. Fitzgerald. Reprinted by permission of Vintage Books, a Division of Random House, Inc.

Farrar, Straus & Giroux, Inc.: for excerpts from "Leda," from *New Poems [1908]: The Other Part* by Rainer Maria Rilke. Translation copyright © 1987 by Edward Snow. Published by North Point Press and reprinted by permission of Farrar, Straus & Giroux, Inc.

The author is also grateful to the following agencies for permission to reproduce the illustrations: the Trustees of the British Museum, the Ministry of Culture of the Hellenic Republic, the Staatliche Antikensammlungen und Gloptothek in Munich, and the Ministero per in Beni Culturali Ambientali and its Archeological Superintendencies in Florence, Etruria Meridionale, and Emilia-Romagna-Bologna.

For Philip
1943–1992
because I loved him
and always will

Contents

List of Illustrations

Cover: Dionysian Procession, detail of a vase by the Niobid painter, Archaeological Museum, Ferrara

Attending to the Gods: Priestesses Attendant on Dionysos, vase painting by the Dinos painter, Archaeological Museum, Naples

Hades: Locri tablet depicting Persephone and Hades, Archaeological Museum, Naples

Hermes: Detail of the Hermes of Praxiteles, Museum at Olympia

Dionysos: Hellenistic head of the young Dionysos, British Museum, London

Apollo: Head of Apollo from the west pediment of the Temple of Zeus, Olympia

Hephaistos: Pelike by the Kleophan painter depicting the return of Hephaistos, Staatliche Antikensammlungen und Glyptothek, Munich

Ares: Aphrodite and Ares as depicted on a red figure kylix by the painter Olios, Museo Nazionale, Tarquinia, Italy

Poseidon: Detail of the bronze statue of Poseidon found off Cape Artemision, National Museum, Athens

Zeus: Bronze head of Zeus from Olympia, National Museum, Athens

Acknowledgments

I want to thank George Lawler, the Crossroad editor whose welcoming embrace of my first book, *The Goddess: Mythological Images of the Feminine,* provided me with the essential initial encouragement without which neither this book nor those that have appeared in between would ever have been written. I want to thank him especially for discerning that this *was* a book, and not, as I had at first imagined, a very long chapter in my *Women's Mysteries.*

I regard these two books as in some sense twins, two books that were (at first unbeknownst to me) gestating during the same period. In another sense I view this book as twinned by William Doty's *Myths of Masculinity.* I am delighted that our books will be appearing at about the same time, with the help of the same editors, and issued by the same press. Our conversations about myth and ritual, about the Greek gods, about women and men, during the many years since we were first graduate students together at Drew and then colleagues at Rutgers University, underlie more of what I try to say in this volume than I could possibly sort out.

I want also to thank Richard Underwood, David Cohen, Philip Loftus, and Peter Wayson for the innumerable ways in which they've helped me toward my own understanding of the gods, particularly of Hermes, Dionysos, and Hephaistos.

The book began as a very tentative lecture presented to the San Diego Friends of Jung. I want to thank them for inviting me to present a woman's view of the masculine in response to my gentle questioning of how they could have planned a whole series on the masculine to include only male speakers when every Jungian conference on the feminine that I knew of had always tended to have at least as many men as women presenting. I want also to thank the men and women who have participated in the workshops I've led at several universities and Jung centers that were part of my preparation for writing this book.

I am grateful to Diedrick Snoek and Patrick Green for welcoming me into the discussion group on "Images of Masculinity" at several of the annual meetings of the Society for Values in Higher Education.

The male students who over the years have taken courses I've offered on the goddesses and on the psychology of women are really responsible for bringing me to realize that, if the Greek goddesses can be so relevant to the experience of men, the Greek gods might also be relevant to the self-understanding of both women and men.

I want to thank Frank Oveis, my other editor at Crossroad, for always knowing when to push me and when to be patient, for writing cover copy and catalogue copy that always seems to articulate what I'm trying to say in my books better than I've managed to, and for his friendship.

As has been true of all my books, this one owes immeasurably to the generous helpfulness of Elaine Rother, not only for all the letters and telephone calls, the duplicating and mailing, she has done directly on its behalf, but even more for the calm and competent way she handles most of the administrative work of the Department of Religious Studies at San Diego State University — thereby making it possible for me to find the time I needed to research and write this book.

A hint of how much I owe to River Malcolm, the woman I live with and love, for helping me toward my way of approaching and responding to the gods is provided in the excerpts from her poetry included in the final chapter.

Finally, I want to thank my father and brother, my former husband and our four sons, for what I've learned from them about men and about the rich diversity of masculinities — and for their love.

July 1991, Del Mar, California–July 1992, Orcas Island, Washington

· 1 ·

Attending to the Gods

Almost twenty years ago in an essay called "Goddesses in our Midst," Philip Zabriskie wrote of the roles played by the goddesses in men's lives.[1] I now find myself pulled to write a parallel piece about the gods in *our* midst, about the gods as they appear to women. It has taken me a long while to recognize the importance of this project.

Somehow it seems that I have always known how much women need goddesses, images of the divine as female, images that recognize the sacredness of the feminine and the complexity, richness, and nurturing power of female energy, images that affirm that the love women receive from women, from mother, sister, daughter, lover, friend reaches as deep and is as trustworthy, necessary, and sustaining as the love symbolized by father, brother, son, or husband. As long as I can remember the goddess figures of the ancient world have provided me, and many other women as well, with images that recognize as integral to a woman's own being not only empathy, intuition, and vulnerability but also courage, creativity, loyalty, and self-confidence, resilience and steadfastness, the capacity for clear insight, the inclination for solitude, and the intensity of passion.

In the book on Greek goddesses I published about a decade ago I was conscious of hoping to write about my own experience of the feminine (or, rather, about the diversity and complexity of female ways of being) in a way that would ring true to other women and was surprised to discover how many men felt I had spoken to them, for them, as well. But it didn't occur to me back then when I was working on that book that we women might also need the gods. Although after its publication several of my men friends asked me, "And when will you write about the gods?" my response was, "I think you men need to do that for yourselves." I still believe that. But now I also believe *I* need to do it – for myself, for women, and also perhaps for men.

In his "book about men," *Iron John*, Robert Bly says that "our obligation – and I include in 'our' all the women and men writing about gender – is to describe the *masculine* in such a way that it does not exclude the masculine in women, and yet hits a resonant string in the man's heart." He goes on to add that "our obligation is to describe the *feminine* in a way that does not exclude the feminine in men but makes a large string resonate in the woman's heart."[2]

My present project honors this "obligation" – and somewhat subverts it. For I don't so much feel drawn to write about the *masculine* (as Bly invites me to) as about energies and modes of presence that Greek mythology represents embodied in male gods. I am less comfortable than Bly seems to be with the essentialist assumptions that make it possible to speak with assurance about "the masculine" or "the feminine,"[3] and so less ready to conclude that male deities would necessarily embody *the* masculine (or even *a* "masculinity," one of several possible forms of masculinity, as William Doty might propose.[4])

I do, however, see these figures as embodying ways of being, "worlds," that enter into the experience of both men and women, and I recognize that these "worlds" differ from those epitomized by any of the goddesses. As Walter Otto wrote of the Greek gods and goddesses:

> None of them represents a single virtue, none is to be encountered in only one direction of teeming life; each desires to feel, shape and illumine the whole compass of human existence with his [or her] peculiar spirit.... Each represents a wholly different but a whole world.[5]

So I am convinced that we need goddesses and gods, need all these images and myths, to help us see who we are and what we might become – for I continue to believe that the psyche needs images to nurture its growth. I also still believe that not only do these ancient mythical figures illumine our lives but also that our own lives, our achievements and failures, our relationships and our dreams, shape and enhance our understanding of the myths. We can each speak of these divine figures only as they have shown themselves to us. Thus my view is *a* woman's view, not *the* women's view, nor necessarily exclusively a *woman's*.

Therefore as I turn now to write about the gods as I have come to know them, I cannot help but wonder anew how much of my experience, my perspective, will be relevant to others, to other women or to men.

The Greeks took it for granted that the gods would enter into the lives of women as well as of men. They imagined Dionysos as present in the midst of the most intensely woman-centered rituals, those practiced by the maenads. They imagined Apollo entering the very body of the Delphic priestess to speak through her to his petitioners. They pictured Hades pulling Persephone down into the underworld and Hermes leading Eurydice back out. They envisioned Poseidon granting a young woman he had raped her wish to be made a man so that she might never be violated again, and Zeus disguising himself as a goddess in order to succeed in his wooing of the beautiful Callisto. They recognized that there are occasions when each of the gods was worshiped by women, was seen as relevant to their inner experience, their most profound needs and hopes, their bitterest suffering, greatest fears. I, too, have come to believe that the gods will from time to time make an appearance in our midst, among women and in women, and that it is important for us to learn how to discern the signs of their presence and to discover what response it requires.

Not that the gods play a role in the psyches of women exactly analogous to the one played by the goddesses in men's inner lives. To affirm that would issue in a circuitous return to animus theory, to the notion that a mostly unconscious male figure serves as the most important soul guide in the inner lives of women, as, according to Jung, an unconscious female figure, the anima, serves to connect men to their deepest selves. I question the neat parallelism, because I remain persuaded that female figures play a more central role in the psychology of most men than male ones do in the psychology of women. Since all of us humans are born of mothers and thus have as our earliest experience of intimacy a relation to a female other, it seems likely that throughout our lives, for most women as well as for men, the most powerful images of wholeness, and of the source of meaning and vitality, will be female. Thus, for women and men alike, the goddesses may touch a deeper chord of experience than the gods do.

Nonetheless, male images do appear in the psyches of women, even if these are not the images that connect us to the most profound layers of our being. Male figures appear in our dreams and in our outward lives, appear with power, power to confuse and transform. These figures may most often appear as counter-players, as other, as ego-alien, but they may also appear from time to time as ego-figures. Women may even have dreams in which we ourselves are men, like a dream I had of being a half-breed Indian youth initiated into becoming my people's Keeper of the Stories[6] or another dream in which I found myself growing male genitals.[7]

Despite my discontent with Jung's contrasexual assumptions, despite my resistance to the androgyny ideal, despite my dis-ease with conventional notions of what constitutes masculinity or femininity, I believe we need to attend to these male figures. I want to find a way of doing this that escapes getting lost in theoretical argumentation or revisioning, but I also want to avoid looking only at particular instances, at clinical cases, at the details of my own experience or that of other women I've known as friends or students or patients. I hope to do this by looking at the Greek gods and trying to discover what I find in them relevant to my self-understanding and to my understanding of what is constellated in me in particular relationships with men (as well as, of course, trying to become clearer as to how these gods may help illumine my understanding of men).

Of course, the male figures that appear in our outer lives

or in our dreams or fantasies will appear in the guise of men we've known, our long-dead grandfather or the doctor who helped us give birth to our babies, the husband we've slept beside for decades or the just-appointed new colleague. Or they may appear as strange combinations of familiar figures, as someone who is somehow both the father of our childhood and the analyst whom we now visit each week, or as both a dearly loved but sorely troubled son and a bit player in a movie we didn't even like. Or we may find ourselves being lectured by a wise old African medicine man or wooed by a charming prince who seems to have stepped right out of the pages of a fairy tale read to us when we were children. Very rarely, perhaps never, will we find ourselves directly engaged by a figure we immediately, unambiguously recognize as a Greek god. But, then, the Greeks too knew that gods almost always appear among mortals in one disguise or another.

It is almost always only in retrospect that one realizes that the god was here. It was Zeus who lay in my bed when I thought I was with my husband. It was Apollo who helped me believe that, even if I had done something truly heinous, it could be forgiven; I could pick up the pieces of what was left of my life and go on. But for me that retrospective recognition brings illumination. To rename my experience, to honor the particular divine power that had made itself manifest, is to discover the sacred meaning-giving dimension of my experience, to discover connections where I had seen disjointed fragments, depth where I had known only triviality. It is also to recognize parallels between my experience and that of countless other humans who have suffered a similar loss, exalted in the gift of a similar blessing. As always it works both ways. An unexpected accident happens that turns my life completely upside down; it seems that nothing like this has ever happened before, and then suddenly I laughingly realize, Hermes is at it again! Or I am reading about Zeus's amorous exploits and reading once again as I have so often before of his coming in the form of a golden rain shower to make love to Danae (whose father had sought to protect her from all lovers by locking her in an underground prison); but on this reading I am drawn to remember how my gentle and knowing golden-haired first lover knew how to reach me through all the father-imposed barriers that had isolated me from lovers and from my own sexuality – and now I feel I understand the myth, understand the penetrating accuracy of its metaphors.

I choose to work with the Greek gods, because I know them, because I grew up with the myths that relate their inter-actions with one another and with human men and women. It doesn't even feel exactly like a choice. These gods are there for me; to construe experience in terms of them feels like speaking the language native to my soul. H.D. begins a poem by asking:

> *What are the islands to me,*
> *What is Greece?*[8]

When I ask myself the same question, the answer is: home, the home of my soul. These are, of course, not the only myths that might challenge and illuminate our own experience, but they are the ones that continue to have the power to do so for me, and perhaps for many others raised as I was in a Eurocentric culture. As Jean-Pierre Vernant puts it:

> The works ancient Greece created are different enough from that of our mental universe to give us a sense of disorientation from ourselves, to give us, along with the feeling of a historical distance, the consciousness of a change in the person. At the same time, they are not as foreign to us as others are. They are transmitted to us without a loss of continuity. They are still living in our cultural tradition to which we continue to remain attached.[9]

I am aware of the dangers of projection in my approach, that I read into these evidences from a long-ago world my own ways of feeling and forms of thought. Certainly, I *want* more than that, want to apprehend another way of organizing, living in, the world that might enhance my own, and thus I seek to understand the Greek perspective in its own terms, but empathicly. Nonetheless, I admit that ultimately I am asking questions about myself, about us.

I'm glad that men have begun to explore their relation to the masculine, and glad that some of them have begun to do so through reflection on the gods of ancient Greece, because they too appreciate that Greek mythology provides richly diverse epiphanies of the masculine. I agree with Hillman and others that the psychology of men has until recently been too much in thrall to the mother and the contrasexual anima. I am impressed by the evidences of how much men have hungered for a psychology that focuses on what fathers and sons (or *puers* and *senexes* — young men and their elders — to suggest a theory even more free of the traditional obsessive focus on the family drama[10]) can give one another. I am moved by how responsive many men have been to the work of Robert Bly, Robert Moore, Eugene Monnick, Sam Keen, and others. (Though I am saddened by how some strands of the contemporary men's movement seem to be radically antifeminist, as, I acknowledge, strands within feminism, particularly in its earlier years, were emphatically anti-male.)

Now I see it as time for us to say how a woman looks at all this, which is differently. I believe consideration of the Greek gods might help women move beyond the limitations of animus theory (which takes contrasexuality for granted and presupposes an essentialist understanding of masculinity and femininity)[11] and toward a careful, precise attending to the various male figures that act upon us and in us. Jung was right in at least one point: the males that figure importantly in women's psyches are plural, not singular. I believe the gods of Greek polytheism will be helpful in this project because they may enable us to sort out this sometimes confused plurality. As these gods take on the roles of brother, father, grandfather, husband, son, or lover, women may discover how each male role constellates a different response in us (and also that there are many different ways in which each of these roles may be embodied, many different ways of being brother, or father, or husband).

And we may find that some of these gods, from time to time at least, move to the center of a woman's experience, become not figures we relate *to* but figures we relate *as*, that we identify with. To try to express this in Jungian terms: a male god may appear to a woman less as an animus figure than as persona, shadow, or even ego. Oddly, careful attending to these male figures, rather than confirming a clear-cut sense of what is masculine and what feminine, may lead us to see how distorting and arbitrary a bipolar view of gender can be.

Although the gods represent energies the Greeks saw as most appropriately embodied in a male figure, they knew no one, male or female, could escape being touched by these energies. That is what the Greeks meant by speaking of these energies as gods, as *theos,* that is, as immortal, permanent, ineluctable aspects of the world.

Each of these gods is truly a *god*, charged with ambivalent power. Each is sometimes helpful, ofttimes dangerous.

Each of these male divine beings, like each of the goddesses, represents a world, a way of ordering all experience, that we shut ourselves off from if we ignore our participation in that world. As Karl Kerenyi recognized, "Each God is the source of a world that without him remains invisible, but with him reveals itself in its own light."[12] I find myself wanting to echo Rilke's plea, "Let no one of the gods vanish. We need each and every one, every one should matter to us, every perfected image."[13]

At the very heart of polytheism lies the conviction that only the totality of the gods and goddesses constitutes the divine world. In all of Greek mythology none of the gods ever denies another's existence – though they may fiercely dispute a particular claim to authority. There are many myths that reveal how fatal it is for us humans to overlook even one, to fail to give each his or her due honor. Though some rituals were gender specific and some gods had only same-sex attendants, no deities were worshiped only by members of one gender. From this perspective, for any of us, man or woman, to disregard even one of the gods or goddesses is to curtail the richness of the world and the fullness of the human. But the realms of these various deities are not logically separated from one another; the polytheistic system is not closed or harmonious. The pantheon is not organized like a conceptual system, but rather like a Mycenaean kingdom,[14] or even more aptly, like a patriarchal family[15] — or rather an anomalous and often dysfunctional family that poses as a patriarchal family. The relations between the gods are fluid, alive; their ever-shifting alliances can be communicated only through story, or rather through stories — and the stories are all interconnected. Freud once said that if one were to follow up on all the possible associations, a whole life could be unravelled through the interpretation of a single dream. Similarly, to follow the trail of any one Greek myth is to find oneself engaged with the whole of Greek mythology, all the stories and all their variants.

For Greek mythology is not just a "mythology of bits and pieces," a "scattered and heterogeneous pantheon," "a mere agglomeration of gods," the product, in random circumstances by virtue of accidents of history, "of fusion, assimilation and segmentation." Rather, the sense of the whole exerts pressure on each of the individual gods, each of the modes of energy, so that "each of these powers becomes distinct not in itself as an isolated object but by virtue of its relative position in the aggregate of forces." Thus the aim of the kind of exploration of the gods that I propose is not to discover our identity with any one of these figures, but rather to be better able to discern when and how each becomes manifest in our experience.[16]

The system can't be learned deductively, nor can the character of any one of the gods. We can't conclude that because Poseidon is a sea god, he will therefore have particular attributes, nor can we gain access to the *who* of the god simply by adding up his epithets or cult titles. Each of these so dramatically anthropomorphic, humanlike gods is an organic whole, truly like a person. And like a person, each appears differently in different times and places. As Lewis Richard Farnell observes, neither in myth nor in cult were these divine personages "pure crystallized products." Nonetheless, the divine name "was a powerful talisman, a magnet attracting to itself a definite set of cult-ideas and legends, and often has a certain ethical-religious character of its own."[17]

And these gods *are* like persons. This seemingly obvious fact needs to be emphasized. For Greek mythology is distinctive in the "almost canonical value" it accorded to "anthropomorphic depiction" in the special status its myths and visual art granted the human body and the human soul "as a mirror of divine power."[18] Nietzsche once observed that the Greek gods "justified human life by living it — the only satisfactory theodicy ever invented."[19] This makes it perhaps fatally easy for us to "read" these gods solely from a psychological perspective, to see them as relevant only to a deepened, more complex self-understanding, and thus to ignore the equally significant ways in which to the Greeks who worshiped them they served to make visible the order inherent in the cosmos and to provide institutional structure to the social realm. Fully to honor these gods thus requires of us that we seek to take into account their pertinence to our involvements with one another and to our relation to the natural world, and not only to our inner lives.

Of course, none of us has access to an unmediated relation to these divinities. We know them primarily as communicated through Greek literature of the classical and Hellenistic world and through the interpretative studies of generations of other scholars. My own understanding of the Greek gods has been deeply informed by classicists like Walter Otto and Karl Kerenyi, who have a gift for apprehending and communicating the character of the various individual members of the pantheon, the character of "what appeared to the Greeks as Hermes"[20] (or Zeus or Dionysos). This is not to say these scholars captured *the* essence of these gods. Otto's Apollo is quite different from Kerenyi's — and mine is different still.

And, of course, even when I find some of their conclusions more expressive of wish-fulfillment fantasy than I feel entirely comfortable with, I have learned enormously from such feminist scholars as Merlin Stone and Charlene Spretnak, who have helped shape my perspective and my questions.[21]

Each of these scholars, and I too, have sought to open ourselves to these gods, agreeing with Walter Burkert that "the language of polytheism can only be learned passively."[22] We must open ourselves to let each god reveal himself.

So as I approach each of these divinities, I begin by asking, "What do I know of this pattern of energy? How has it entered my life? Do I know it mostly through interpersonal relationship? Or as something I also know inwardly, as part of my own complex and always still in-process wholeness? Is it alien, pulling me away from my "real" self? Or only apparently alien but somehow uncannily familiar? And of course, I know that some of the gods who are my familiars may be another's strangers, and that perhaps others will recognize only as embodied in another an energy I know as active within myself.

I want to learn what happens as I become more specifically, consciously aware of the particular differentiated energy associated with this god, or with that one. How does recognizing this god, this mode of energy, this pattern of behavior, this particular mode of sacred power help me become aware of dark hidden urges and fears, of ignored suffering, and of how to get in touch with my hitherto unhonored strengths? Jung said that the gods have become our pathologies, but he too knew that they can still be more than this, can still act in us in healing or transformative ways. As the Jungian scholar Rafael Lopez-Pedraza expresses this insight: "The interest of a psychology based on the archetypes is to look through a situation in order to encourage psychic movement rather than to reduce the patient's condition to its mythical counterpart."[23] The Greeks knew that each of their gods had fearsome and beneficent aspects. Any real engagement with them will make this evident to us as well.

As I have learned more and more about the Greek divinities — partly through further research, partly through continued reflection, partly through new dreams and new experiences, I have come to see some of the goddesses differently than I did ten years ago when I wrote *The Goddess,* have come to view some of the gods and goddesses differently than I did in my *Myths and Mysteries of Same-Sex Love.* Burkert supports my sense of the appropriateness of such a shifting, ever unfolding response. Because the Greek pantheon is not a closed or harmonious system, because it remains unstable and full of gaps, it provides, he suggests, "an inexhaustible impetus to intellectual creativity, albeit more in the style of the poet than the thinker."[24]

My method of engaging these mythological figures is clearer to me now than it was a decade ago. I love the classical literature, the clearly defined shapes the gods and goddesses have in epic poetry and tragedy where telling a tale involving any one of them immediately lets us know which one it *must* be. I value the spiritual depth of the Platonic dialogues and of the mystery religions. But I have become ever more appreciative of the perspectives of the early preliterary strand, more attentive to the clues we have to a period when Greek myth was still *myth,* not art, more fluid, more chthonic, more connected to a matrilineal world, more like other people's myths — more like them also in its relative obscurity and inaccessibility. I am more aware of wanting to be fair, of recognizing the need to look at how the *gods* (and not only the goddesses) appeared in this more ancient stratum of the traditions. For it seems fatally easy to see these male deities only in their most defined, Olympian, patriarchal aspects.

In my exploration I will look only at the major gods, the Olympian gods — but not only at their Olympian aspects. The briefest survey reveals immediately that many of the gods, all to some degree, were there in what we know as Greece either well before the Dorians and Ionians came or else arrived with these invaders but became the gods that Homer describes only through interaction with cults devoted to the indigenous goddesses and male gods. Once we're attuned to this possibility, we see signs of it everywhere, in the material evidence of vases, inscriptions, sculpture and architecture, and, more veiledly, in the cult-epithets, the rites and myths of the historical period.

Farnell's magisterial five volumes, *The Cults of the Greek States,* give us a lively sense of the many different elements that go into the making of a god. We come to appreciate how the rituals associated with a particular god (and thus the very perception of the god) varied from one locale to another. We also come to understand that prayer and sacrifice were always offered to a particular aspect of the god or a particular local-ized epiphany, never to an abstractly universalized version. Indeed, the point of oracles was often to instruct the peti-tioner what name or epithet to use as he or she addressed the divine.[25] To use the wrong name obviated the possibility of any favorable response and might actually make things worse. Farnell also helps us begin to grasp how much more clearly differentiated from one another these deities were in litera-ture than they ever were in cult. Indeed, the cultic traditions attest to a fluid overlapping among the divinities much more like what we find characteristic of Egyptian mythology than I would have imagined could be true of "my" Greeks![26] The Linear B tablets show that, although by 1600 B.C.E. the names of many of the deities who were later to be seen as consti-tuting the twelve Olympians were already known in Greece (including Zeus, Hera, Poseidon, Athene, Artemis Hermes, Dionysos, perhaps also Ares and Aphrodite, but probably not Hephaistos) – the supreme deity was still Potnia, the divine mistress, the great goddess known by many names. Though the *names* of the other deities were already known, they were not yet the gods and goddesses described by Homer.

Indeed, I have come to recognize more clearly than before the degree to which the clearly ordered Olympian pantheon with Zeus at its head is a creation of Homer (or perhaps in part of his antecedents among the bards), as Nilsson's lifelong study of the Mycenaean origin of Greek mythology led him to conclude. Only in Homer, Nilsson asserts, are the Olympians *the* Olympians, dwelling together on the mountain top. In cult each deity still mostly continues to have his or her own place. Even after Homer, Zeus still does not have a supreme position in cult, only in myth. Zeus is given his supremacy by the poets, not by a politically dominant group whose god he was, nor, as in Egypt, by priests whose speculations led to the articulation of a henotheistic theology.[27]

I have already indicated my recognition of how helpful looking at the gods may be for men. I would like to add that I believe it's not enough just to discover the more differentiated, complex, polytheistic view of maleness that comes from attending to the differences among Homer's Olympians. To add the perspective of the earlier traditions about a pre-patriarchal masculinity, about a maleness not defined by an opposition to the goddess, suggests an even more fluid understanding of gender — which reappears in some of the mystery religions. This is also highly relevant to women's relation to the gods, for it makes it so much easier to recognize these gods as inner energies, as living in women not just as our "masculine" side or as pertinent only to deepening our understanding of the men with whom we interact. How much easier once we move beyond (or behind) the bipolar assumptions of the later periods for women to recognize the moments when we look *through* the gods rather than just *at* them.

Jane Ellen Harrison claims that though the "making of a goddess," the process of the transition from local heroine to pan-Greek goddess, is mostly lost (because of the intrusion of the patriarchal system and its focus on descent through the male line), we *can* trace the process that leads from local cult-hero to male god. She notes the important role played by adjectival cult titles in the "making of a god." The indigenous divinities were, she believes, originally venerated local human heroes who (because of the "primitive" tendency to avoid using the actual name of a dead person) become nameless gods addressed by cultic epithets. Only the Olympian gods, the gods of the invaders, had proper names that defined and crystallized the divinity addressed. These late-appearing gods absorbed the powers of the more ancient deities by adding their cultic titles to their own names. Thus, for example, the chthonic snake deity of archaic Attica, Meilichios, disappears and in his place stands Zeus Meilichios, Zeus Easy-to-be-entreated.

"Whether a local hero became a god depended on a multitude of chances and conditions, the clue to which is lost. If a local hero became famous beyond his own parish, the Olympian religion made every effort to meet him half way." We can see a variety of patterns. No pains, for example, she says, were spared to affiliate Herakles. He was made Hera's child by adoption, married to Hebe, welcomed to Olympos after his death. Yet, "always elaborately entering, he is never really *in.*" At some places the process of absorption issued in a compromise: at Amyclae, for instance, the worship of Apollo is superimposed on that of Hyakinthos. The altar to the god sits atop the tomb of the hero, who is now known as the mourned mortal beloved of the god. Elsewhere, myth (or guilt) betrays evidence of a more violent suppression, as at Delphi where Apollo is acknowledged to have seized the oracle from Gaia.

Harrison helps us see the conservative tenacity of ritual and how it works to preserve that which on the surface has been overcome. And even on the surface we are talking about a gradual process of superimposition. There was no one big event through which the Olympians conquered their predecessors[28] — which is not to posit a smooth evolutionary continuity nor to deny the radical differences between the prehistorical Mycenaean world and the Greece of the city-states.

To understand the process whereby the Greek gods came to dominate over the goddesses who were the predominant deities in pre-Olympian Greece and to become the figures we know, we must look at cult and not only at myth; we must look at art and architecture and not only at literature. These evidences of popular culture also offer us more insight into what the gods meant to their female devotees than do the literary texts that give us direct access only to the patriarchal perspectives of the elite.

Vincent Scully has helped me see how dramatically architecture makes these religious transitions visible. The architecture of the Indo-European bands who arrived in Greece before 1600 B.C.E. makes clear that these early Mycenaean kings saw themselves as ruling under the protection of the great goddess. But unlike the Minoans of the more archaic culture of Crete, they built directly on the goddess's hills, not below in its shelter. Scully concludes that these Bronze Age lords "actively wished to worship the goddess but inherent in their sense of lordship was a competition for her place." They "wanted it both ways," wanted her protection *and* a recognition of their own heroic glory. "Something tense and revolutionary must have been felt as the lords mounted the goddess' hill." The Mycenaeans battled against her and yet, as Scully sees, through the inevitability of their death, she in the end defeated them. This in turn gave new sanctity to the already sacred places where their death occurred. Their tombs became the focus of the later hero cults and thus indirectly transmitters of the earth goddess's power.[29]

The later Dorians, who arrived in Greece around 1000 B.C.E., on the other hand, tried to curb the power of the ancient goddess. Refusing the comfort of her womb-tomb, they proudly burned their dead rather than burying them and thus relinquished "the hidden promise of immortality the old traditions granted." They attempted to subjugate the goddess to their own lordly Zeus. Nature is now conceived as hostile to human will and desire, and a new tension between the human and the natural order is introduced.[30]

By the time of Homer each of the gods and goddesses was regarded as the "embodiment of a certain kind of natural and/or psychological force." Though the Olympian gods had not created the world (that had been the work of earthmother Gaia and her immediate offspring, the Titans), they (who differ from us only by virtue of their power and immortality) are the quintessential expressions of its nature. This new perspective (which Scully sees as particularly manifest in some of the temples dedicated to Apollo) emphasized the differences between humanity and nature, humans and the gods. "But," he says, "the old way of peace was never entirely forgotten, although its forms had at first been thrust brutally underground, so that a strain of haunted memory was henceforth to give a further dimension to Greek thought" – and this strain (and perhaps even a new reconciliation) can, he believes, be discerned in some of the late classical temples dedicated to Zeus.[31]

Greek temples of the classical era, as Scully shows, explore and praise the character of a god or group of gods in a specific place that is itself felt to be holy and that is experienced as embodying a particular deity as a recognized natural force. It is the site that first suggests the presence of the god. With the construction of the temple "both the deity as in nature and the god as imagined by men" are represented.[32]

Scully's sensitive, exact descriptions of the temples dedicated to the Olympian gods correlate with my more intuitive response to these temples. He has helped me understand that it was not some strange racial memory that led me to recognize a mother goddess's subliminal presence at Delphi when I first went there before I knew of its association with any deity but Apollo. The temple's relation to the site was *intended* to convey that Apollo's presence had been superimposed on Gaia's. Scully has helped me trust that the sense of Poseidon I receive from watching the sun set at Sounion is as reliable as what I could learn from any handbook.

Learning how to "read" the evidence of architecture and sculpture, cult-epithets and cultic rituals, enables us to watch how the old persists, how it modifies what is brought in later, how it reappears more plainly in the late classical period. The gods are all of these various versions of them – are in a sense all the various stages of their development at once. No particular account of a god is the "real" one.

Thus I know how important it is to respect the chronological unfolding, to understand the historical development, but I also understand Walter Otto's love of the clearly and poetically shaped classical representations as in some sense "archetypal" – and I have come to a better appreciation of Karl Kerenyi's deceptive, graceful moving back and forth among all the different strata of the tradition as though they all existed at once, spatially rather than temporally.

As I turn, one by one, to the Greek gods I begin by looking at the stories, not at some handbook's more abstract notion of what each god means. The god *is* the stories that are told about him, the rituals that are celebrated in his honor, the temples dedicated to him. That's where the juice, the illumination lies. To discover the meaning of each of these gods to women, means, of course, paying special attention to the tales told about his involvements with goddesses and with mortal women, and also to the rites in which women participated – though we would miss much if we looked only at those elements of the tradition. We need to heed also how these gods interact with one another and with mortal men, and even to the rituals in their honor in which only men might participate.

A full exploration of the meaning of these gods would entail examining all the myths and rites associated with each divinity and all their variations. It would mean examining all the attributes and epithets, cult titles and poetic appellations. It would also require a careful examination of the variegated ways in which each god is associated with every other. For we must never forget that these deities are part of a pantheon and that therefore, as Jean-Pierre Vernant reminds us, it is the pantheistic structures, not the gods in isolation, that make visible the ordering pattern through which the Greeks imagined the natural world, human society, and the individual psyche.[33]

I've not done that. I haven't been passive, receptive, patient enough to allow each to fully reveal himself. There is much about each of these gods I don't yet know. What I can present is inevitably only a view from along the way. Nor have I given each equal due. For now, at this particular juncture of my life, I am more attuned to some than others. And because this book is about how these gods move on us and within us, on me and in me, I can't order my exploration in a more programmatic way. Nor can I do it in a logical order. I have to do it in my order, a psychological order, an order different from that of the handbooks, which usually proceed by order of rank or genealogical succession — and different, too, from another woman's order, or probably any man's.

· 2 ·

Hades and Cronos

I must begin with Hades, because he got me into all this, with a dream within which, after announcing that it was time to go in search of Her, I found myself in Her presence in a dark cave deep under the earth.[1] The dream led me back to the Greek mythology I had loved as a child and to Persephone, the goddess of spring with whom my mother had taught me, her spring-born daughter, to identify. The amplification of the dream led me to another Persephone, the dread goddess who rules in the underworld, who was abducted there by its lord, Hades. So I have always felt that he abducted me along with her — abducted me into my immersion in the underworld of Greek mythology, into the world of the goddesses and the gods, and into those times of deep reflection on my own life that have been part of that immersion.

I begin with Hades as he appears in the familiar tale, the tale of his abduction of Persephone, as presented in the old and beautiful ritual poem, "The Hymn to Demeter." At the outset Persephone and a group of lovely young maidens are gathering flowers and bedecking each other with garlands and wreaths in a springtime meadow. Her companions don't even notice as Persephone wanders off to pick an especially beautiful large narcissus and is accosted by a dark stranger who leaps forth from a chasm that opens in the earth, wraps his arms about her, and carries her down to the darkness from which he had come. The hymn focuses on the mother's grief and rage when she learns of her daughter's disappearance and on her fruitless search to reclaim the maiden. Possessed by her loss, Demeter too is abducted to the underworld, albeit less literally. Eventually she persuades Zeus to intervene, and he sends word to Hades that Persephone must be allowed to return to the upper world. But because the maiden has eaten several pomegranate seeds while in his realm, her release is conditional on her coming back to spend part of each year with him. Nonetheless, the poem ends with a moving evocation of the joy with which the two goddesses greet each other at their reunion.

This is almost the only story in Greek mythology involving Hades, and yet he hardly appears in it. We see him only as the dreadful god whom Demeter experiences as an intruder and despoiler. The hymn gives us no sense of what this episode means to him, of his motives or feelings, and little of what it means to Persephone. We know only that she becomes Hades' bride and goddess of the underworld and that she and her mother come, as "The Two Goddesses," to preside over the Eleusinian mysteries, the rites whose initiates were freed of the fear of death.

The story stirs the imagination of almost all who hear it. Greek rituals associated with it recognized its relevance to the cycle of vegetal life, to the human fear of death and hope for immortality, to the deep bonds that exist among women, particularly mothers and daughters. Some of these rituals were open only to women; others also included men. The myth seems to have particular resonance for women, and many of us feel that in some sense it is *the* myth for us, as the Oedipus myth may be *the* myth for men. Yet we find many different meanings in it.[2] Some of these retellings focus, as does the hymn, on the beauty of the mother-daughter bond, others on the devouring narcissism of Demeter's love for her daughter; some have seen it as a rape story, others as a tale of sexual initiation. The abduction is variously seen as signifying that Persephone is being taken from her mother or from her connection to the matristic world, from an outgrown role as dependent daughter or from the superficial upperworld of ego concerns to the realm of soul.

Of course, the different interpretations include very different assessments of Hades. For some readings he is almost beside the point, an intruder in a scene that has no place for him. Some see him only in negative terms; others as a creatively transformative figure. Perhaps the ambivalent response befits a lord of the underworld, a god associated with a realm that inherently inspires so much intense fear and longing. (I say this because like Freud I do believe we wish for death as well as dread it, that the fantasies of cessation, completion, of all tension and struggle being over are deeply compelling.)

Hades feels more important than the hymn allows him to be. Or, rather, it leaves us wanting to know more about him, as though the clue to reading the story well might lie in knowing him better.

For help, I turn to the other evidences available to us, and immediately discover how sparse they are. There is little art — a few beautiful reliefs and vases showing him with Persephone, peaceful scenes of "loving intercourse" where the two are pictured dining together. (These depictions are often paired with representations of Demeter and her daughter also sharing a meal, a pairing suggestive of a reconciliation between Hades and the mother goddess.) Farnell notes that most pictorial representations don't seem to know the myth of Hades as ravisher, and Mylonas notes that those that show Persephone being carried off do not portray her as showing terror or anxiety. Both wonder if perhaps only Demeter views him as rapacious intruder, if perhaps the point of the story is to move us beyond that perspective.[3]

Perhaps Hades is not often shown because he is the invisible and unnamed god. His name, Aidoneus, itself signifies that he is, by definition, the unseen one. Although Aidoneus is, most probably, the god's oldest name, it is nevertheless one rarely used, perhaps because it evokes the terror associated with the dark, unlit realm over which he rules, the House of Hades. Farnell says this name remains taboo, barren; it was felt to be unsuitable for use in invocations. Mostly the Greeks sought to sublimate their terror of the underworld god by invoking him with other more euphemistic names, such as Trophonios, the nourisher, Polydegmon, the receiver of many guests, Euboulos, the good counselor, or Ploutos, wealth-giving. Many of these titles are intended to suggest that Hades is not only the grim god of death but also a god of the fruitful harvest – as though he were a male counterpart to Demeter and not only to her daughter. We may understand this renaming as signifying aversion, denial, but it may also bespeak a deeper truth, a truth not only about Hades' possible origin as an archaic chthonic fertility deity but also a recognition of an inner fruitfulness that immersion in his world may yield.

There were only two temples dedicated to Hades: one at Elis, which was open on only one day a year and then only to the priest, and the other at the entrance to the Eleusinian temple complex. This sanctuary, very different from the free-standing marble temples dedicated to other Greek divinities, is little more than an entrance to a natural cave carved out of the hillside. An opening in the cave floor was regarded as an entrance to the underworld – not the entrance through which Hades first brought Persephone down to his unlit realm but perhaps the gate through which she passes each year as (during the celebration of the Mysteries) she comes up from the underworld and then returns. The location of the temple there, at the outskirts of the place where the mysteries were performed, says much about how Hades is perceived. He belongs to the story, but only peripherally, only to its preparatory phases. This reminds me of how in my dream of going in search of Her, I dismiss the kindly wise old man who offers to help me: "You and I have been through this before." Earlier I had needed his help; now what was to happen involved only me and Her.

There are no cults in which Hades plays a central role. There is no period in Greek ritual life in which he is important. There are no records to indicate that he was known to the indigenous people before the Indo-Europeans arrived. In Homer, where there is little recognition that the realm of the dead is sacred, he is almost ignored. And later, in both myth and rite, he is little more than Persephone's shadowy consort. The world of the dead is again ruled by a goddess, as it seems to have been long before it came to be viewed as under his rule. Yet he is still *there* and the place bears his name. Like Hestia, he seems to be absorbed by his place, to be more place than plot or story.[4]

Though there is no evidence of Hades' presence in prehistoric Greece, there is also no evidence that he was brought into Greece by the Aryans, along with Zeus. Nevertheless, like Zeus, he enters Greek mythology as one of the sons of Cronos. According to Hesiod, almost immediately after his birth Hades (like his sisters, Hestia, Demeter, and Hera, and like his brother Poseidon) was swallowed by his father (who feared that some day one of his progeny would seize power from him as he had seized it from his father) and remained in his father's stomach/womb (the words are the same in Greek) until rescued by their last-born sibling, Zeus. A variant version relates that Cronos, rather than swallowing his newborn sons, threw the infant Hades into Tartarus (the ancient name for the deepest recesses of the underworld, for the withinness of the earth, and thus perhaps for the womb of Gaia) as he threw newborn Poseidon into the sea.[5]

◆

I would like to pause a moment to explore more fully the relevance of Cronos to our understanding of Hades. Hades, so the most familiar story tells us, was separated from his mother and enclosed in that male womb almost from birth – or, as the alternate version relates, already in infancy was cast into the underworld. Each of the five swallowed siblings responded differently to that traumatic starting-point. The others eventually make their way *out,* whereas Hades remains forever in a dark enclosed space – and thereby perhaps reveals that he is more truly Cronos's child than any of the others. (Iconic representations of Cronos combine Hades' features with those of Zeus, as though he contains within himself attributes his sons divide between them – for Zeus inherits his father's role as chief among the gods, Hades his underworld identity.)

Cronos, the father, remains forever in an even darker, more

enclosed space than Hades, the son – not in the House of Hades, the place just below the surface of the earth where the souls of the dead live remembering (and re-member-ing) their lives above, but in Tartarus, which lies as far below the surface of the earth as earth lies below heaven. This place of punishment, which, so it is said, no ray of light ever penetrates, is inhabited by exemplary sinners, like Ixion and Tantalus and Sisyphus, who once dared challenge the gods' sovereignty and now endure eternal punishment, and by the Titans, that is, by Cronos and the other male members of his generation of divine beings who were sent there by Zeus after he succeeded in seizing power from them.

The story of the overthrow of the Titans is clearly at one level the story of the overthrow of a more ancient race of gods, that is, of the displacement of an earlier cult by a later one. The story hints at the existence in preinvasion Greece not just of goddesses but of male gods. The vivid, concrete stories told about these gods in the opening pages of Hesiod's *Theogony,* stories of castration and cannibalism, incest and monstrous generation, clearly seem to derive from an early stratum of the tradition, not to be original inventions. The Titans represent a generation of gods closer to the natural world than the later Olympians. Oceanus, for example, is a river god; Hyperion, a god of the sun. Cronos's sickle indicates his connection to vegetal fertility – which perhaps destined him to be also viewed as a chthonic god, an underworld deity. His closeness to the original mother goddess, to earth-mother Gaia, is shown by his coming to Gaia's aid when she protests that Ouranos forces her to keep her children, the Hundred-handed Ones and the Cyclopes, within her body (Tartarus), though she is long since ready to give them birth.

Thus because of his allegiance to his mother, Cronos, her youngest son, is pulled into a rivalry with his father that sets in motion an ever-reappearing competitive rivalry between father and son, brother and brother – and that eventually leads Cronos to be so concerned about his own autonomy that he turns against even Gaia. Thus Cronos feels himself torn by that conflict which to some degree all of us children of the mother experience: the tension between longing for her protection and blessing and wanting to establish our independence of her.

In accordance with his mother's plan, Cronos severs his father's genitals and releases the imprisoned creatures from their confinement in her womb. But once he has assumed his father's place as chief among the gods he puts the Hundred-handed and the Cyclopes right back in Tartarus — and, as we saw, eventually ends up there himself, enchained, enslaved, because Gaia (and the female Titans as well) come to Zeus's aid against Cronos when Zeus in his turn sets her monstrous offspring free once again. The cultic correlate of this is that in the historical period as a dispossessed, enslaved god, Cronos becomes a god worshiped by slaves.[6]

But there is another version of Cronos's ultimate fate. Among the Orphics Cronos was said to have eventually been reconciled with Zeus and to be ruling now on the Isles of the Blest rather than enslaved in Tartarus. The time of his long-ago rule on earth is seen in this tradition, not as a wild, barbaric period, but as a golden age, a time of peace, justice, prosperity, an era before men knew oppression or labor, as an Eden that, of course, couldn't last on earth in the "real" world.

Taking account of these alternative visions, H. S. Versnel suggests that Cronos represents both frightening chaos and utopian freedom.[7] He sees this as evident in the Kronoia, a saturnalia-like ritual still celebrated in late classical times, during which the position of slaves and their masters was reversed and the temples of all the other gods were closed. The closing of the temples signifies, he suggests, that "the contact with the gods currently ruling is broken; the pre-Olympian era returns temporarily. It is precisely Kronos's mythical character as god of primordial times that explains his presence in the un-cultic vacuum between the times. He represents an embodiment of primeval chaos in its dual aspect of freedom as a joy and freedom as a threat."[8] "Kronos' era is the pe-

riod of giants, creatures with a hundred hands, monsters and
Cyclopes.... Kronos does exist but only in mythical times:
before the present reality (during the primeval era) or after
it (death) or at the outermost edges of this reality." Cronos
"disappeared from active cult and became a 'mythical' god
and... *consequently* was considered to be a representative
of the mythical era before history proper, which began with
Zeus and the Olympians."[9]

How well this accords with Freud's identification (in
The Interpretation of Dreams) of the Titans with our most
primitive energies, energies that no matter how thoroughly
repressed can never be killed off. Almost a hundred years earlier August Wilhelm Schlegel, in his *Lectures on Dramatic
Art and Literature,* had suggested a similar interpretation of
Cronos and his siblings:

> The Titans, in general, mean the dark primary powers of na-
> ture and of mind; the later gods, what enters more within the
> circle of consciousness. The former are more nearly related to
> original chaos; the latter belong to a world already subjected
> to order.[10]

In general, the Greeks imagined that after Zeus came to
power Cronos and the other Titans were safely put away,
either in Tartarus or on the Isles of the Blest. But there is an
Orphic tradition that they reappear on earth one final time. At
Hera's instigation they emerge to seize the infant Dionysos;
they tear him to bits and then proceed to feast on his dis-
membered body. Luckily Athene arrives on the scene in time
to save the child's heart, which she then feeds to Zeus. Later
the child god is reborn of Zeus's own body. More immediately, Zeus kills the Titans with his lightning bolt, and, so the
Orphic anthropology claims, it is from the Titans' ashes that
we humans are fashioned. The story betrays its late dating,
its misunderstanding of ancient ritual. For in cult those who
kill and eat a god are always his votaries, not his enemies. But
in its fantasy of the Titans as powers who may still intrude
upon our world, it speaks a kind of truth, as does its vision of

us humans as carrying an inheritance from these daemonic beings in our very bodies.

Psychologically speaking, the Titans seem to represent the most deeply buried layers of our psyche, layers which nevertheless from time to time erupt into consciousness; they are "id energy" coming into personified form, instinctual energy becoming psychical manifestation. I am struck that in Greek mythology it is the *male* Titans who are relegated to Tartarus. The female Titans, among them Rhea, the prototypical mother of the gods, Themis, goddess of the natural order of things and later of communal order, and Mnemosyne, goddess of memory and mother of the muses, continue to perform their functions in the Zeus-ruled world. The powers that most threaten civilized, human life are envisioned as male. What strikes me most about Cronos is his ruthless readiness to destroy both his father and his sons, his wish to annul past and future, to *be*, without parent or issue. In this he seems to represent a primal life urge that lies even deeper than eros, the urge to connection, and that is paradoxically a death urge, a denial of all other life. It is thus fitting that Cronos would end in deepest Tartarus *and* that he is nonetheless immortal. I feel I understand why the Greeks would imagine this urge as a male urge, though I also recognize its workings in my own life.

The myths about the Titans offer us a salient reminder that we should not identify the unconscious as *per se* female. There are aspects of the unconscious that seem to call for representation by male figures. In *Beyond the Pleasure Principle* and *Civilization and Its Discontents* Freud speaks of two primal cosmic forces, Eros and Death, and identifies them as twin Titans. Though their names do not literally appear on any Greek listing of the Titans, the designation seems appropriate. In both Hesiod and the Orphics Eros (who — *pace* Jung — was always known as a male deity) is recognized as a primordial deity, not as the effete son of Aphrodite we may be more likely to think of. Interpreters of Freud have often rendered what he called simply Death as Thanatos, a woefully inadequate rendition. (Thanatos was a minor deity whose sole role was to help carry the already dead to the underworld.) If we need a name, Cronos would be by far a more appropriate one.

◆

Hades is not Cronos, but he is Cronos's son. And just as Zeus is Cronos's son because he takes over his role as leader of the gods, so Hades is Cronos's son because he takes over his role as a male deity of the underworld. But Hades is a less violent, less self-assertive figure than his father, and often seems to exist less as a god in his own right than as the shadow-side of Zeus.

According to the most familiar myth, after Cronos's overthrow the three Olympian brothers divided the world among them by lot: Zeus received dominion over the heavens, Poseidon over the sea, and Hades over the underworld. Of the three, Hades is the least clearly distinguished. Farnell describes a relief that pictures all three: Zeus is identified by his lightning bolt, Poseidon by his trident, Hades only by virtue of the *absence* of any individualizing attribute and by his averted face.[11]

Kerenyi suggests that perhaps there were *three* major Olympian gods because there had been a triple goddess — the triad of maiden, mother, crone, represented in the later strands of Greek mythology by Persephone, Demeter, and Hekate, but once simply the three aspects of *the* goddess whatever name she might go by in a particular locality.[12] Probably to begin with, he suggests, Hades was only the dark chthonic side of an otherwise bright god. Farnell believes Hades may have been created as a male counterpart to Zeus, to assure that patriarchal rule would be recognized as extending over every domain, including even the underworld. Thus to begin with Hades may not have been an independent god but simply an epithet of Zeus — the unseen side of the all-seeing god. The Greeks, at least subliminally, seem to have known this.[13] For among Hades' many other names, we find him spoken of as "another Zeus," as Zeus Chthonios, the underworld Zeus, or, more apotropaically, as Zeus Meilichios, the mild and gentle Zeus.

Indeed, in the tales about Demeter and Persephone Hades, Zeus and Poseidon seem to keep taking each other's place. In the most familiar version Zeus slept with Demeter (who longed to have a daughter to whom she might give the motherly love of which she herself had been deprived when her father swallowed her immediately after her birth) and fathered Persephone (but was not allowed any access to his daughter by Demeter, who wanted the girl to be hers alone). Hades was Persephone's abductor and, later, husband. But even in "The Hymn to Demeter" it is acknowledged that he took the daughter with the father's permission, so that the invisible uncle comes as a kind of father-surrogate, the hidden side of the incestuous father. In the Orphic Rhapsodies the incest theme becomes more manifest: Zeus first rapes his mother Rhea/Demeter and fathers Persephone, and then in the form of a snake (Zeus Meilichios) rapes his daughter Persephone and fathers Dionysos.[14] According to another tradition Poseidon rapes Demeter who turns into a mare to escape the god but is caught by him as he assumes the form of a stallion. Demeter then gives birth to Despoina (a cult title meaning "mistress"), who seems to be essentially another Persephone. Kerenyi believes that there was once a now-lost tradition of Demeter's own abduction to the underworld.[15] All this suggests how easily Demeter and Persephone take one another's place (confirming Kerenyi's sense that the mythologem is about the way in which mothers have daughters who become mothers who have daughters and so on and on in an ever-repeating circle), and, more relevantly to my purpose here, how easily Hades slips from view and has his place usurped by Zeus.

Later, Hades is also often identified with Dionysos, especially in the Orphic tradition, where Dionysos is regarded as both lover and son of Persephone. This absorption somewhat mitigates the terror associated with Hades as an independent god and serves, as the euphemistic cult titles also do, to emphasize his relation to vegetal fertility. Herakleitos, too, tells us that "Hades and Dionysos are the same," as the way up and the way down are the same. Kerenyi believes that the identity between Dionysos and Hades was known but veiled by the author of "The Hymn to Demeter" who set Persephone's rape in the Nysan field.[16] And although George Mylonas is adamant about Dionysos not having any role in the Eleusinian mysteries, even he admits that by the third century B.C.E., especially among the Orphics, the distinction between Dionysos and Hades, between Dionysos and Iacchos (the child whose birth was announced at the climax of the Eleusinian rite), was no longer clear.[17] Although some scholars have understood the "sameness" of Dionysos and Hades to signify the existence of a covert death wish in the midst of life, I find persuasive Veronique Foti's suggestion that it implies a recognition that Dionysian passion resembles initiation into the domain of Hades in the midst of the passionate fullness of life, a glimpse of a different kind of life, one not constrained by social role or social convention.[18]

Mostly, however, as we have seen, Hades is the unseen god, the god who never emerges from his underworld realm and even there is not the most significant figure. He emerges on that one occasion to abduct Persephone and *perhaps* on one other occasion. (There is a tradition that he received so painful a wound while battling Herakles over Cerberus that he had to go to Olympos to be healed by Paian, the physician to the gods.)

I still see Hades' abduction of Persephone as meaning something different from rape; I see him as meaning something different to me than one who violates my body or my soul. I note how many of the gods seek to force themselves upon one woman after another — we shall see how this is true of almost every other of the gods except for Dionysos — and that Hades reaches only for this one. And Ovid, at least (though with Ovid one is never quite sure when he is serious and when not), believes that Hades came for Persephone after having first seen and fallen in love with her and then having received permission from her father. (Granted, even Ovid admits Hades did not have, nor would he ever have received, permission from Demeter.) Nonetheless, according to the Homeric hymn grandmother Gaia came to Hades' aid by causing that beautiful narcissus to spring up, as though she saw the necessity of the daughter's separation from the mother. In Ovid, too, we are given an image of Orpheus succeeding in persuading Hades and Persephone to allow him to lead his young bride, Eurydice, back out of the underworld by singing a song that recalls the intensity of the love that had first brought these underworld deities together.

I sometimes even wonder if their marriage was sexually consummated (though I recognize all the sexual symbols in the tale, the narcissus and the pomegranate), for on every other occasion that I know of when a Greek god had intercourse with a female, divine or human, a child was conceived,[19] and there is no tradition of this couple having a child. It's true that at the climax of the Eleusinian mysteries there seems to have been a joyful cry announcing the birth of Iacchos; but this is a truly mysterious birth: we know nothing of this child beyond the cry.

Nor is Hades an abductor even of the dead. He does not bring death — Artemis and Apollo do that — nor does he bring the dead or the living to the underworld — Thanatos brings the first, Hermes the second. Hades *receives* those who come; he welcomes them. He neither judges nor punishes, for in his house all receive the same welcome.

I see Hades as representing the impossibility of an all-female world forever immune to intrusion by the male. Demeter had sought to keep her daughter with her forever, to protect her from all contact with the masculine. Persephone *reaches* for the narcissus as she later reaches for the pomegranate. There is some spark essential to her becoming herself, becoming the goddess of the underworld and not just Demeter's daughter, that the relation to Hades makes possible. His temple is outside the sacred precincts, his power in the underworld becomes subordinate to hers, his role is in some ways minor — and yet essential. He helps get something started that might otherwise remain barren.

I think of how different Persephone is from Ereshkigal, who is so lonely, so cruel, so unhappy; I think of how different the House of Hades is from the Sumerian Land of No Return — and I suspect it is because the god Hades is there.

Reflection on Hades leads me to wonder anew, what pulls us away from identification with mother and the mother role, or away from the good daughter role? What pulls us to underworld experience, to a particular kind of underworld experience? For me Hades is the name for that in me which pulls me to engagements with my inner self that consciously I long to resist and yet that I find to be the times of real soul-making. What happens when I get there happens between me and Her, but he helps get me there.

· 3 ·

Hermes

Though Hades serves as a good name for the seemingly alien but unconsciously longed-for pattern of energy that most often pulls me down into the underworld, it is Hermes who leads me back up. Not that his is the best name for all the ways in which I make my way back to reinvolvement with my concerns in the everyday world. Demeter, Aphrodite, and Athene are names for other modes of return, as are Zeus and even Apollo. For what pulls me back may be a resurgence of concern for my children and their children, or the reawakening of passion for another or for my work, or a renewed awareness of my ineluctable involvement with the human community. But perhaps these gods and goddesses don't really get me out of the underworld, don't come down to get me, can't reach me there. They are rather gods whose power I rediscover as I find myself re-emerging. And those deities affect my life in many ways, not primarily as psychopomp; whereas it is as psychopomp that I have most directly experienced Hermes.

I think particularly of the period in my late thirties when I found myself so overwhelmed by guilt and loss that I could no longer even imagine that things might ever be different. I had stopped dreaming. I had lost all touch with that in me which hopes, which could imagine love or joy. It felt as though my soul had died, was lost somewhere deep in the underworld. It seemed evident to me that there was nothing in me that could pull me back up. When I wrote of this time in *The Goddess,* I said that eventually I discovered there is a natural healing process, an end to such experience that we do not make happen, but that comes. Now I would say a god did it; Hermes appeared. When my despair was at its greatest I felt that the only possible resolution was for my body to join my

soul in death. The winter solstice was approaching. I flew
to a faraway seaside city where the ocean waters that I have
always loved, always recognized as the source from which
life emerges and to which it must return, would be warm. I
had planned to dive into those waters and swim until I could
swim no further. But during the night of my arrival I had
a dream, the first in many, many months, in which I bled to
death aborting a child. And, magically, when I awoke there in
a chair across the room sat my dearest friend, who had divined
what I was up to and borrowed money to follow me to this
far distant place simply to say, "You cannot go without saying
goodbye." The dream, I would now say, was sent by Hermes,
god of dreams, and my friend who helped me to understand
the dream as signifying, not that I should go ahead with my
plans but that the dream death, the symbolic death, was death
enough – that friend was sent by Hermes also, or (as it felt)
was Hermes.[1]

Hades saw Hermes as an ally, one who could move back
and forth between the upper and lower worlds as he could
not. And so in order to make some contribution to the
Olympians' battle against the Giants, Hades lent his cap of
invisibility to the messenger god (who later lent it to Medusa-
slaying Perseus). Occasionally, Hermes is himself invoked as a
god of the underworld. For example, Aeschylus's *Choephoroi*
begins with Orestes' invocation: "Oh Hermes of the nether
world, administering a power given thee of thy father, be my
saviour and my helper at my prayer." But the context makes
clear that Orestes is here asking for help with an earthly activity. In chthonic cult Hermes is given a more subordinate role.[2]
Hermes may wear Hades' cap of invisibility, but he wears it
with a difference: it enables him to be suddenly and magically
present, to thieve and trick.

Hermes knows ways down to the underworld that make
return possible. In mythology it is he who guides those
who in the midst of life approach the underworld with the
hope of return, Odysseus, for example, and Orpheus. Rilke's
poem "Orpheus. Eurydice. Hermes" poignantly portrays how

grieved this "god of speed and distant messages" is when Orpheus's impatience and doubt prevent his being able to bring
Eurydice back out of the underworld with him:

>   *Abruptly*
> *the god put out his hand to stop her, saying,*
> *with sorrow in his voice: He has turned around —.*[3]

Homer's slain heroes (who see the afterlife only as not-life)
find their way to the underworld without Hermes' assistance
(though Hermes helps Priam retrieve Hector's body from
Achilles so he might give his son the ritual burial that alone
will gain him safe access to the land of the dead). Participants
in the mysteries, who believed that the life of the soul might
be a more real life than earthly life, went to Hades under the
tutelage of deities other than Hermes.[4]

Thus Hermes guides us to a particular mode of underworld
experience. We turn to him when we want to learn from and
make use of underworld experience, to turn it to advantage,
to find the luck hidden in it. I don't believe that an outer Hermes necessarily appears in male guise, but I wonder if, when
women feel they want a male therapist, they may, perhaps
unconsciously, be looking for the kind of guidance Hermes
provides. (I recall that I chose to work with a particular therapist, to whom I'd earlier been introduced in casual social
circumstances, after having a dream in which he appeared.
I was walking down an empty, dark urban street. Suddenly
from behind my left shoulder he appeared, wrestled me to
the ground and ran off with my purse. I woke realizing how
wonderful it would be to have a guide with such power to
take me by surprise.)

Reflection on Hermes' role as psychopomp leads us to
think about underworld experience in a particular way, to
ask: What is the difference between being guided to rather
than abducted to the underworld? What is the difference between spending time in the underworld and being stuck in
it? (I think of Theseus and Perithous going to the underworld

with the rash project of abducting Persephone from it, being welcomed by Hades and invited to sit on the Seats of Forgetfulness and ending up stuck there forever.) What is my experience of being led back out? What in me knows how to make use of underworld experience, to turn loss into gain?

Hermes is there in those moments when one suddenly discovers one is not in control, when everything turns upside down. So much of depth psychology is dedicated to bringing us to recognize the correlations between inner and outer, to acknowledge how much we have actually helped shape or have invited that which seemingly happens *to* us. Hermes teaches us another lesson: that we can never after all protect ourselves from having things happen to us, from chance, from surprise, from the god.

According to the Homeric "Hymn to Hermes," when Apollo first discovers that his infant brother, Hermes, has stolen his cattle, he threatens that unless the child quickly tells him where his cows are

> *I'm going to take you*
> *and throw you into black Tartarus,*
> *into a hopeless darkness.*
> *What a terrible end!*
> *And neither your mother*
> *nor your father*
> *will bring you back to the light of day!*
> *You'll wander under the earth,*
> *leading little people around.*

But by the end of the hymn, the two are reconciled and Apollo announces that from now on Hermes will be "the only recognized messenger to Hades. " The poem ends by telling us:

> *And Hermes mingles now*
> *with all men and gods.*

And even though
he helps a few people
he cheats an endless number.[5]

Somehow Hermes as psychopomp and Hermes as thief, trickster, cheater belong together. When we speak of Hermes in
relation to "underworld," we must think not only of the souls
in Hades but of the Mafia, of gamblers, thiefs, pickpockets,
pimps — the shady side of life. We must think of what Jung
had in mind when he invoked the "shadow," the unloved, dis-
reputable side of ourselves, as a soul guide, as a figure who
may lead us from identification with persona or ego to a more
holistic sense of self.

Hermes is called upon as a guide to the underworld not
only by those who hope to go there purposively but also by
those who fear it. Greeks kept images of Hermes in their bed-
rooms and petitioned him to send them sleep but not death,
for they saw him as the god not only of the transition from
life to death but of the analogous transition from day to night.
Hermes puts the wakeful to sleep and awakens the sleeping.
The last libation before one retired for the night was offered
to Hermes in hopes that he might send a lucky dream.

Hermes is also invoked by those who fear ghosts as one
who might keep them away. Thus he is invoked when libations are poured to the dead and charged with the care of
graves. Very likely the *herms,* the ithyphallic pillars dedicated
to Hermes set up at crossroads and at the entry to every house,
were also originally intended to ward off the spirits of the
dead.

Hermes' connection to the underworld suggests a connection as well to the pre-Olympian world, as though he might
also serve as a transition figure between the old gods and the
new. Indeed, in some traditions Hermes is a child of Ouranos rather than of Zeus.[6] And Kerenyi says that as we learn
more about Hermes, his portrait deepens "towards the Titanic": "We sense in him the essence of the pre-Olympian
world." Kerenyi sees the emphasis on the lucky accident, the

windfall, the *hermaion*, in the traditions about Hermes as "a residue of the chaotic primordial condition.[7] Otto, too, finds in Hermes' relation to magic (and in his ithyphallic aspect) a reminder of the Cronos era.[8]

Indeed in cultic history Hermes was probably originally a pre-Hellenic god from Arcadia. All sources seem to agree that Hermes begins as a heap of stones, a *herm,* marking a boundary or a crossroad. As Burkert notes, "It is amazing that a monument of this kind could be transformed into an Olympian god."[9] It is also fascinating to watch the process whereby an immovable boundary stone becomes surrounded by tales about boundary transgressions and the breaking of taboos. The aniconic origin testifies to Hermes being a very early divinity. He is the herm. He is also the crossroad itself. Every threshold is Hermes. When silence falls in a conversation that, too, marks Hermes' presence. He is *there,* at all transitions, marking them as sacred, as eventful, as epiphany. Our awareness of Hermes' presence opens us to the sacredness of such moments, of those in-between times that are strangely frightening and that we so often try to hurry past. We never really know what may lie on the other side of any threshold. I think particularly of the moments of silence that may fall in the midst of a conversation with a beloved friend, when eye is locked into eye, and one suddenly realizes how all the words have been evasions of this moment when soul gazes directly into soul.

There were few temples to Hermes, an indication on the one hand of his subordinate status, on the other that he was felt to be *there,* "wherever people lived and died. Through Hermes every house became an opening and a point of departure to the paths that come from far off and lead away into the distance."[10]

Like many other chthonic deities Hermes was born in a cave. Though in all likelihood originally a god of fertility and death, he is associated more with a pastoral than a settled agricultural world, as the ram he so often carries on his shoulder bears witness. This also fits in with his messenger role, for it seems to be part of Hermes' nature not to belong to any locality, not to possess a permanent abode.[11] Hermes is Mercury, mercurial, quick and changeable. To know Hermes is to know that in ourselves, that in another, which is not fixed, reliable, stable — and to honor just that instability as divine.

Hermes' name appears in some very ancient Attic cults, including the Thesmophoria and the Eleusinia, but always as a subordinate god. It seems likely that this subordination was part of the systematizing process whereby the ancient gods were replaced by newer ones. We note in the Homeric hymn how Hermes seduces Apollo and Zeus into accepting him despite his thievery and perjury, his very un-Olympian behavior. Apollo becomes Hermes' big brother and hands over to him all his own earlier associations with the chthonic realm, with fertility and with the dead. In the hymn Hermes also becomes one who sacrifices to the other gods, and trickily inserts himself among them by dividing the sacrifice into twelve portions and allotting one to himself.

Hermes' status as a servant of the gods suggests that he was originally the god of a conquered people.[12] Like Cronos he, too, is the god of a festival where slaves and masters exchange places. Hermes is also honored at another festival during which thievery is permitted.[13] Hermes' association with a suppressed culture explains why he has to be subversive, tricky, a cheat and a thief. As Freud understood, the repressed has to disguise itself to get past the censor. The dream, the hysterical symptom, the slip of the tongue, the thing forgotten or misplaced — all these "compromise formations" are Hermes. He tricks me into betraying myself, and then stands there as the one who sees through the tricks and helps me learn not only to acknowledge the hitherto unacknowledged wishes as my own but, more importantly, to delight in the trickiness, to come to love the complexity of the psyche's modes of expression, its poetics.

Hermes is the archetypal self-sufficient, primordial child — a precocious, enchanting child god who steals from Apollo and lies to Zeus so charmingly that they don't even feel like losers afterward. That the Homeric hymn to Hermes shows him as this beguilingly playful child suggests that his child aspect is an essential, perhaps the essential, aspect of this deity — another hint that in the Olympian Hermes we find an echo of the pre-Olympian world in its utopian golden age aspect. In the hymn Hermes tells the tale of his own conception — as though in a sense he'd been there, even before his parents met, as though his existence were not dependent on theirs. Hermes is also the only son of a nymph among the Olympians, another indication of his being between-the-worlds; all of the other Olympian gods (except Dionysos, another special case) are sons of goddesses. (Nymphs are immortal females associated with various aspects of the natural world, of lesser status than the goddesses and often represented as their attendants; those with names and stories like Hermes' mother, Maia, were probably originally local goddesses.)

When Hermes is invoked as "the friendliest of gods to men," we sense that he comes from a time when the gods and humans were not so profoundly separated from one another by the gulf between divine immortality and human mortality as they have come to be in the post-Homeric period. The difference between gods and men, the divine immortality of the gods as contrasted with the finite mortality of humankind, so important to Apollo, is of little import to Hermes.

Hermes' connection to the chthonic realm makes him a god connected not only to the realm of the dead but also to fertility, expressed in the concrete way of early religious symbolism by his phallic aspect. The most common iconic representation of Hermes, as we have already noted, is the ithyphallic herm, the always erect ritual penis, the penis of fantasy, of undiminished power. Kerenyi sees the Hermes' connections to generativity and to death as closely related: "As source of life the phallic is related to soul. . . . In other words, seed is also soul." He notes that Priapos, the minor fertility god endowed with enormous genitals, was like Hermes also a grave-guardian, and that in the mysteries of Samothrace the herm was regarded as the symbol of immortality. Kerenyi sees this as related to a view of immortality, for women as well as men, which places it "under the aspect of the active, the masculine,"[14] that is, a view of the afterlife that sees it as a *life*, as *new* life – not just the persistence of the old life, not just a re-emergence of what already was, but the appearance of something genuinely novel.

But, of course, the phallus is also a sexual symbol, though Hermes' phallus is the emblem of a distinctively Hermetic sexuality – an earthy, we might almost say smutty, sexuality. In Hermes there is always this conjunction of the spiritual and the shameful, this discovery of the sacred in the rejected and the disavowed; there is always contradiction, paradox.[15] His is an active, "audacious" sexuality,[16] a sexuality based not so much on love or even passion as on an enjoyment of the adventure, the stolen love, the seduction, the game of love, the trickery, the conquest. Lopez-Pedraza recognizes that for Hermes the fantasies of love are really more important than the consummations. His sexuality is very much in the imagination, is a *psychic* sexuality that delights in its polymorphous perversity.[17]

As Kerenyi puts it, the feminine for Hermes "is nothing more than an opportunity." Kerenyi also sees that, conversely, "for the primal woman [Hermes] was only an impersonal masculinity, almost a toy." Here we have a clue that Hermes was at one time simply the consort, the sexual servant, of the goddess, that he was called into the world by the primordial Great Goddess, perhaps in her manifestation as Hekate, the female divinity most like him, goddess of the underworld and of fruitfulness.[18] Kerenyi, retelling the story of Hermes coming upon Persephone playing in that by now familiar meadow and getting an erection, suggests we might take this as our best clue to the meaning of Hermetic phallicism: "the first evocation of the masculine principle through the feminine."[19] Hermes discovers his masculinity through being aroused by the goddess. Somehow, though, I cannot imagine Hermes as ever entirely in the goddess's power. It is rather as though he *allowed* her to use him. Hermes is, after all, the one who is able to warn Odysseus about how to protect himself from being destroyed by his entanglements with Circe and Calypso — and yet also teaches Odysseus how to enjoy the time he will spend in their company.

This introduces the theme of Hermes' relation to women. There are, of course, no wives. One could no more imagine a faithful Hermes than one could a faithful Aphrodite. Although there are many nymphs whom this son of a nymph seduces, and many mortal women, the most important and most revealing stories about Hermes' love affairs involve his relation to Aphrodite. Each has fantasies about the other. Homer tells us that when all the gods discover Aphrodite and Ares under the net the cuckolded Hephaistos had devised to catch them making love, Hephaistos is enraged and embarrassed, and Poseidon is scandalized, but Hermes is ready to announce that *he* wouldn't mind making love to Aphrodite with *all* the gods and goddesses looking on, even if there were three times as many chains shackling him to the bed.[20]

In the Homeric "Hymn to Aphrodite" Aphrodite pretends to Anchises that she has been brought to him by Hermes against her own will. She relates to Anchises an elaborately detailed fantasy that begins with the familiar scene of a group of maidens playing in the meadow. In her imagined version of this scene it is Hermes who appears in the women's midst and carries one (herself, of course) away; though Hermes comes not as a rapist or even on his own behalf but rather to bring her to Anchises so that she might be this mortal shepherd's wife and bear his children. Anchises is not deceived by Aphrodite's image, nor had she meant him to be. But it is a truly Hermetic fantasy, one that delights in the playful side of lovemaking.[21]

So many of my mentors, my teachers, my soul guides, have acknowledged their debt to this god: Freud for whom Hermes signified the possibility of going into the underworld and emerging with a boon, with a life-giving interpretation; Jung for whom he was primarily Hermes Trimestigus, the patron god of alchemy, of transformation; Thomas Mann, particularly in the persons of his two most charmingly guileful protagonists, Joseph, son of Jacob, and Felix Krull.[22]

But I am particularly intrigued by the shape-shifting role played by Hermes in the life of Hilda Doolittle, the Imagist poet we know as H.D. One of her first published poems, based on a poem included in the *Greek Anthology,* is called, "Hermes of the Ways."

> *More than the many-foamed ways*
> *of the sea,*
> *I know him*
> *of the triple path-ways,*
> *Hermes,*
> *who awaits.*
> *Dubious,*
> *facing three ways,*
> *welcoming wayfarers.*
> . . . .
> *Hermes, Hermes,*
> *the great sea foamed,*
> *gnashed its teeth about me;*
> *but you have waited,*
> *where sea-grass tangles with*
> *shore-grass.*[23]

The poem was written to disentangle the complicated, ambivalent feelings she felt toward her friend since childhood Ezra Pound. She showed it to him, along with one or two others, one afternoon when they met in the British Museum. He took a pencil and pared her lines to give them the stark simplicity of the poem we know; he scratched out her signature and replaced it with her initials, H.D. She came to feel that he sought to make H.D. as Imagist poet *his* creation. She saw him as Hermes the thief, who brought up to the world, made public, what was not yet ready to be shown; he stole her poetry.[24] For many years after that initial creative spurt during which she wrote in the ways he had encouraged, she wrote hardly at all, or, rather, almost nothing that she was willing to make public. Most of what she did write and felt she could not publish, novels and some poetry, was dedicated to the attempt to explore the soul meaning of her pull to women.[25]

Then almost fifteen years later she entered analysis with Freud. He too was a Hermes, but one who gently encouraged her own exploration of the underworld and her reemergence. She knows that others have seen him as a thief:

> STOP THIEF! But nothing could stop him, once he started unearthing buried treasures (he called it striking oil). And anyhow, wasn't it his own? Hadn't he found it? But *stop thief,* they shouted or worse. He was nonchalantly unlocking vaults and caves, taking down the barriers that generations had carefully set up against their hidden motives, their secret ambitions, their suppressed desires. *Stop thief?*[26]

But she recognized as treasure the trash "that a ragpicker would pass over in disdain," the old attic-stored junk that Freud helped her to retrieve.[27]

> Our Professor stood this side of the portal. He did not pretend to bring back the dead who had already crossed the threshold. But he raised from dead hearts and stricken minds and maladjusted bodies a host of living children. . . . It was the very love of humanity that caused the Professor to stand guardian at the gate. . . . He would stand guardian, he would turn the whole stream of consciousness back into useful, into *irrigation* channels.[28]

Freud helped her to see that her deepest desire was for a union with her mother, for a return to a female source, that only thus could she win free of her submissive relation to Pound, to Aldington, to Lawrence, men who still held her creative spirit in thrall though she had long ago broken off any outer-world connections with them.

On the other side of her analysis H.D. could recognize the Hermes in herself. Hermes, the Hermes of the Greeks and of the alchemists, became her patron, alchemy her metaphor for artistic creation. She was herself the thief whose poetry plundered long discredited sources to validate female experience and vision. She saw her poetry as an alchemical reactivation of a seemingly dead patriarchal mythological tradition, a reworking of misogynist myths to reveal the Mother who always stood behind them.[29] Her last book, whose title suggests that now she has claimed "H.D." as her own creation, is entitled *Hermetic Definition.*

Some scholars view Hermes as himself a *feminine* god. Ginette Paris, for example, says he is "a god who is male by sex but feminine in spirit." She speaks of him as embodying a restless, intuitive, situational intelligence that relies on the flash of insight — a mode of consciousness otherwise characteristic of such female figures as Aphrodite, Pandora, Ariadne, Medea, Circe, and Athene.[30] Of course, I too recall that Hermes' gift to Pandora, the original woman fashioned by Hephaistos and then endowed with "all gifts" by his fellow deities, is to invest her with lying and crafty speech and a deceitful nature; that is, Hermes makes her in his own image. It seems to miss the point, though, to call this "feminine" (as it is, to my mind, beside the point to call Athene's rational acumen and assertive courage "masculine"[31]). Hermes isn't "feminine"; he is, precisely, Hermes, not Apollo or Zeus, and some of those of us who experience Hermes acting through us are women, some men.

The children of the major gods serve to bring into focused view some particular aspect of their divine parent. Thus to know the god, it helps to know the child. Included among the offspring of Hermes is thieving Autolycus, the grandfather of Odysseus. According to the story, once long ago both Hermes and Apollo fell in love with a beautiful maiden named Chione. Apollo waited for night to fall before pressing his suit, but Hermes put her to sleep during the day and made love to her forthwith. In due course, she bore Autolycus to Hermes and another son to Apollo. How apt that the issue of a stolen love should be a thief.

It works the other way around as well: to know the god it

helps to know the parents. There are diverse traditions about the parentage of many figures in Greek mythology, each true, each revealing a particular truth about the offspring. Thus Pan, though usually considered a child of Hermes, is sometimes also spoken of as a son of Ouranos or of Cronos, or Zeus, or Apollo. When Hermes is Pan's father, the mother may be a nymph, the daughter of Apollo's son, Dryops — or (*horrible dictu!*) "faithful" Penelope! Half-human, half-goat, Pan is an ithyphallic pastoral god who represents the boundary between animal and human, nature and civilization. (A parallel tradition makes Hermes the father — and the son! — of Priapos.)

There are even more different traditions about the origin of Eros. According to Hesiod Eros is a primordial deity, as old as Gaia herself. The most familiar genealogy regards him as the son of Aphrodite and Ares. There is, however, also a tradition that Eros was parented by Aphrodite and Hermes. There is little dispute, however, about the parentage of Hermaphroditos — the name gives it away. (Although some say that Hermes tricked Aphrodite into yielding to his embraces, which sounds likely enough. Kerenyi even cites a tradition that makes Hermes and Aphrodite twin children of Ouranos[32] — and surely luck and love belong together.) In any case their son Hermaphroditos grew up to be one of the most beautiful youths ever born, so beautiful that the nymph Salamacis fell obsessively in love with him. Like a Narcissus or a Hippolytos, the comely youth refused her every advance, but she leapt upon him after spying him bathing in a stream and clung to him with such devotion that their bodies fused into one. The youth was horrified but the change was permanent — and liberates our imagination from understanding identity only along the fault line of gender antithesis. Hermaphroditos tricks us — is this a man? a woman? a straddler of the boundaries? a dissolver of them?

But then with Hermes such questions always arise. As Lopez-Pedraza puts it: "He marks the boundaries of our psychological frontiers and marks the territory where the foreign, the alien, begins in our psyche."[33] Otto says that the essence of Hermes is luck, "the favorable moment and its profitable exploitation." Hermes teaches us "to see the divine in roguery and irresponsibility — accepting both gain and loss as a favor of the god."[34] And Kerenyi ends his book by concluding: "For all to whom life is an adventure . . . he is the common guide."[35]

Hermes is present when things just happen, in gifts that come to us unsought and undeserved. In my own experience these are the most blessed gifts of all, the ones that lead us to ask after the name of the god whom we should thank. I think of my lovechild, my luckchild, the unplanned first daughter after four planned sons. All that just comes to us, at night in our dreams or by day in our unexpected encounters — that is Hermes.

All sudden givings . . . and all sudden takings away — for Hermes is bad luck as well as good; he is a thief, a liar, a cheat, completely unreliable, the guide who also leads astray. And just that makes him a god. Just that reminds us that there *are* gods and we are but mortal humans. He is the messenger of the gods and ofttimes poses as interpreter of their messages. We learn to listen — and be wary. For words always have more than one meaning. I try to remember always that even Zeus came to delight in Hermes' lies, to see them as adding to the joy of the world.

Hermes the trickster works on me but also in me. Those moments when I feel I've been betrayed, stolen from, those are he, but so also are the moments when the sociopath, the rulebreaker, in me comes to the fore, when I rely on secrecy, cunning, luck. Again I touch on the duality that is always associated with Hermes. This trickster aspect can seem but light and trivial; it can seem destructive and pathological. But this trickster is also a psychopomp, or, rather, Hermes as psychopomp is trickster, light and serious at once. His presence reminds us that the crossing of every threshold is a sacred event. Hermes is associated with all boundaries — and with their transgression. He teaches that the violation of taboos may be a creative act, that to accept the importance of boundaries is not necessarily to be bound by them. Hermes moves back and forth between the worlds.

Otto's portrait of Hermes is still the one that moves me most deeply. He knows him as "gay and at the same time darkly mysterious," speaks of him as "the mystery of night seen by day." When Hermes is present, "It is as if nocturnal mysteries were stirring in broad daylight."[36] When I repeat these words, I think of the beautiful relief at Naples where Hermes is shown gently touching Eurydice to lead her back to the underworld, and I think of Praxiteles' statue at Olympia of Hermes as a gently smiling youth, holding the infant Dionysos at his shoulder.

· 4 ·

Dionysos

The two gods Hermes and Dionysos are as intimately and paradoxically connected as the sculpture (which represents one as a self-possessed adult and the other as a vulnerable infant) suggests. Whereas Hermes transgresses boundaries, Dionysos dissolves them. Where Hermes tries to hide his origin outside the Olympian world, Dionysos flaunts his.

Dionysos is a god who is always arriving and whose arrival is always experienced as threatening, as overpowering, as *epidemia.* Because Dionysos *is* a force that is always new, though actually an ancient deity, he always appears as the stranger — the unwelcome stranger, the persecuted stranger.[1] Because myth after myth describes his arriving as a foreigner and relates the opposition his appearance provokes, scholars at one time assumed he was, indeed, a late arrival in Greece. Today the consensus is that he was there in Greece long before Olympian Zeus. The myths about his being driven away as an unwelcome intruder are now understood as based on rituals in which the king drives the dying god to the sea that he might be reborn, rituals that testify to Dionysos's origin as an ancient chthonic deity. The situation in Euripides' *Bacchae,* where Dionysos is both an unknown stranger and Theban-born, captures the paradox exactly. As Burkert observes, in the Hellenic world a god who dies is "always felt to be foreign. . . . Cultic reality, however, remained a rich conglomerate of Olympian and Chthonic elements."[2]

Most scholars now agree that Dionysos was probably originally a Minoan fertility god, a son of the great goddess, whose cult was for a time eclipsed and when revived coalesced with elements drawn from rites associated with similar Thracian and Asian deities. When Zeus was brought to Crete, his cult absorbed that of an indigenous god whose myth seems at many points indistinguishable from that of Dionysos. Eventually the incompatibility between what Dionysos and what the Greek Zeus primarily mean was felt as so great that Dionysos had to reappear as a separate deity. The Zeus of Homer has been stripped of these Cretan elements and is a very un-Dionysian Zeus. Indeed, Dionysos himself does not play a major role in Homer's epics, where the notion of what makes a god a god seems radically incompatible with what makes Dionysos Dionysos. Nonetheless, the major elements in the mythic tradition associated with Dionysos are alluded to in Homer: the birth to Semele, the liaison with Ariadne, the opposition of Lykourgos — as though precisely to make it clear that this is a different god, a god radically different from the others. . . .

But as we shall see when we consider Zeus at the end of this book, Cretan Zeus and Dionysos are barely distinguishable from each other. In fact, Kerenyi asserts, "they are not separate at all," and might best be given the name "the Zeus-Dionysos of Crete."[3] Both Dionysos and Cretan Zeus are associated with the vegetal cycle; both are born in caves and nursed by women not their mothers.

Even the god's name makes the connection evident. The first part, *Dio,* derives from the same Indo-European root meaning "god" as does the name *Zeus.* The meaning of the second part is less clear; it may include a reference to a place name, though one that, when we try to locate it, as Harrison notes, gets "pushed farther and farther away to an ever more remote *Nowhere.*"[4] *Nysa* does not mean "son of," though, of course, in later tradition Dionysos *is* identified as a son of Olympian Zeus. According to these sources Dionysos is the child of a mortal mother, the Theban princess Semele, daughter of Cadmus and Harmonia, a human child who *becomes* a god, like those other sons of Zeus by mortal women, Asklepios and Herakles. Unlike them, however, Dionysos comes to be not just a god, but a major figure in the Olympian pantheon, the only god among "the Twelve" to have a mortal mother.

That, of course, is the later "official" version of Dionysos's genealogy, one that seeks to minimize the salience of his matrilineal heritage. In earlier Phrygian tradition, however, Semele is no mere mortal but a powerful earth goddess, a chthonic deity closely akin to Persephone. And in the Orphic tradition Dionysos is the child of Zeus and of Persephone herself. In another early tradition Dionysos is the child born to Ariadne (a chthonic goddess in the ancient Minoan world) in the underworld, a child of which he is himself the father.

Thus, to begin with (in the earliest layers of mythic and cultic tradition) Dionysos is the son of a goddess. The story of the Theban Semele's being burnt to death when Zeus (at his mistress's request) makes love to her in his lightning bolt aspect may well be a patriarchally inspired revision of an older tale about a *hieros gamos* between the thunder-smitten earth and the sky.[5] The revised version's depiction of Zeus then arranging to rescue Semele's not yet viable child from the holocaust and having the fetus implanted in his own thigh (or belly/womb) both acknowledges and disavows this truth. As Dionysos becomes "the twiceborn god," he is adopted into the Olympian pantheon. The story gives him a patrilineal heritage to replace the original matrilineal one.

Nor does the mother disappear from the tale. For Dionysos *is,* as Harrison affirms, the son of his mother and represents that role within the pantheon. She suggests that the Semele-Dionysos mythologem mirrors the mother/child relation even more adequately than does the Demeter/Persephone one, for in her view the two Eleusinian goddesses stand to each other less as mother and daughter than as two stages of a woman's life, whereas Semele and Dionysos are clearly parent and child.[6] So for Dionysos to be Dionysos his relation to Semele must be kept in view. Even in the version where Semele dies her fiery death and goes to the underworld, when Dionysos comes to maturity he sets out to rescue her; he descends to Hades, brings her back with him and succeeds in installing her in Olympos, where as mother of a god she rightfully belongs. Thus Semele's status as a goddess is dependent on Dionysos. Her role in myth is simply that of mother of the god, of this god. The myth focuses not on a mother's love of her child (from which he, like Persephone, might be imagined as longing to be free) but rather on a son's undying love of his mother.

Thus Dionysos remains a son of the mother and was, indeed, himself also often called "the womanly god." The story of his rescue of Semele involves an episode in which he, a male god, allows himself to be penetrated, to be treated sexually as a woman. The myth relates that Dionysos, having difficulty finding one of the hidden gates to Hades, is finally given directions to the entryway near Lerna by an old shepherd who exacts a promise that after the successful completion of his mission, the god will allow the herdsman to make love to him. After taking Semele to Olympos, Dionysos returns to fulfill his pledge. Alas, his benefactor has long since died and so the god whittles a large phallus out of fig-wood and lowers himself upon it. There are hints that in the mysteries celebrated in the god's honor at Lerna adult men allowed themselves to be penetrated, as though on the other side of being assured of their identity as penetrators, it might be important to come to terms with their vulnerability and thus achieve a truly whole masculinity.[7]

That is, among the many boundaries this god confounds is that between masculinity and femininity. He may be represented with an enormous phallus (as are the male members of his retinue, the satyrs) or be shown carrying a detached phallus. He may be called *phales,* the phallic one, or *pseudanor,* the man without true virility; he is referred to as *dyalos,* the hybrid, and *arsenthelys,* the man-woman. He is a male god in whose realm submission signifies access to a particular kind of power.

Kerenyi even has the audacity to suggest that the story of Dionysos's birth from the thigh of Zeus is really a euphemistic substitute for an older tradition about Zeus's self-emasculation. The underlying myth about a voluntary castration he sees as symbolizing "the eternally necessary self-sacrifice of male vitality to the feminine sex and hence to the human race as a whole."[8] There are, indeed, many artistic representations of an emasculated Dionysos, a Dionysos without the phallos.[9] There is also a tradition that after his birth from Zeus's thigh, because still in great danger of Hera's jealous wrath, Dionysos was secretly sent off to be raised by the nymphs of Nysa and for a time at least brought up as girl (at Hermes' suggestion) in hopes that this might deceive the goddess. Even as an adult Dionysos sometimes wore womanly garb in a deliberate parodying or confusion or obliteration of gender roles. The *zoe,* the life force, which Kerenyi sees as the essence of the god, is pure libido, not distinctively male or female, active or passive.

Dionysos is not only said to be a "womanly" god but is also a god worshiped in rituals open only to women. The nurses of his childhood become the god's mythical attendants, the Maenads. In historical times as well, actual women, the wives and mothers of Delphi and Attica and Crete, participated in maenadic rituals that took them from their homes and from their domestic roles. Men were excluded and those who dared to spy on them were (at least in legend) castrated or killed. The celebrants formed a ritual community, a *thiasos,* and so were also known as Thyiades; they worshiped the god as a group, not as solitary individuals. On the mountaintops in the company of one another and the god, they allowed themselves to experience their own pent-up instinctual energies. This energy is their own; it could be experienced most fully and freely in a context where men were not present, yet it was the male god, Dionysos, who made possible its release. The women were *en theos*, possessed by the god. Temporarily at least they *were* the god Bacchae. But, despite the name maenad, they were not mad. Those who recognized Dionysos as a god, as a sacred energy that demands recognition, experienced exhilaration; only those who denied him went crazy as the god, despite their resistance, took over.

Some scholars have attributed the prominence of women in Dionysos's cult to women's greater susceptibility to emotion,[10] others to the fact that the god's greatest gift was freedom and women's lives were the most constrained.[11] But it would seem truer to say that it is central to Dionysos to bring release to women, as he brought it to his mother. Rather than thinking of Dionysos in terms of an unbridled sexuality, I suggest we should think of him as devoted to women — to their in-their-selfness, not their social personae. Alone among the Greek gods Dionysos is never accused of seduction or rape or even infidelity: he is Ariadne's constant spouse.[12] He does not violate women; he brings them to themselves.

We might wonder why a *male* god is represented as having this power to bring women in touch with their instinctual nature. My sense is that this communicates that when women are among themselves, emancipated from the receptive and nurturing role expected of them in heterosexual contexts, they may discover an *active* sexuality that is their own, a sexuality that encompasses an obsessive insistence on its own expression that may move into the kind of aggressivity symbolized in the mythological tradition by the maenads frenziedly dismembering kids or fawns with their bare hands and then feasting upon them. Dionysian passion is focused simply on itself; there is no other.

I have known such passion while making love with a lover whose identity was for that moment beside the point, obliterated, but my most compelling experience of Dionysian ecstasy came on an occasion when, so it seemed, only the god and I were present. It was at the time of the summer solstice, on a sun-filled afternoon on the patio of a home I had just moved into. The house was on Serpentine Drive; I had just finished working on the paper on Ariadne that eventually became a chapter in my book on the goddesses; the man I identified as "my" Dionysos in that chapter had sent me a long-treasured vial of pure Sandoz lysurgic acid to use in a ritual blessing of my move. A dear friend had come to join in the celebration with me, but when the god came I was only very subliminally aware of his presence as a witness at the other end of the patio. What happened involved only me and the god. Even now I have difficulty describing it. I was simply lying there in the sun; I was not masturbating; I was not

touching myself nor being touched by another. But I was suf-
fused with sexual energy that completely possessed me and
left me utterly, *perfectly,* satisfied.

H.D. has a poem called "The God," written in response to
D. H. Lawrence's impact on her, which captures something
of what I felt:

> *In a moment*
> *you have altered this beneath my feet,*
> *the rocks*
> *have no weight*
> *against the rush of cyclamen,*
> *fire-tipped, ivory-pointed*
> *white;*
> *beneath my feet the flat rocks*
> *have no strength*
> *against the deep purple flower-embers,*
> *cyclamen, wine spilled.*[13]

The rituals dedicated to Dionysos involved an ecstatic
merging with the god otherwise foreign to Greek religion. It
was this — not his association with the old chthonic themes —
that made Dionysos seem an alien god no matter how long
he had been around. As Harrison notes, the advent of the
dying/reappearing Persephone was never viewed as forcible
entry.[14] Dionysos represented a threatening loss of self as she
did not. (Perhaps another way of marking the violence associated with Dionysos's entry was to make him a great-grandson
of that other supposedly Thracian god, Ares — by way of Harmonia and Semele.) Kerenyi sees Dionysos's connection to
ecstasy as the clue to what Dionysos *is,* the most naked form
of *zoe,* the biological life force, absolutely reduced to itself.
"Where Dionysos rules, life manifests itself as boundless and
irreducible."[15]

Dionysos is a god who appears with the goddess. But to
understand Dionysos we need, as Harrison sees, to understand why this particular son of the earth was adopted by

Zeus, when so many others disappeared or were relegated to the status of heroes or, at best, minor deities. Her answer supports Kerenyi's understanding of the god: it is because Dionysos represents the power of intoxication. "Intoxication is of the essence of the god Dionysos, it is the element that marks him out from other gods."[16] Nilsson agrees: What is distinctive about Dionysos is not fertility but ecstasy.[17] Dionysos is related to all vegetal fertility, but especially to wine. Dionysos is "the male correlate of Kore," Persephone, — "but changed, transfigured by this new element of intoxication and orgy."[18]

The experience of being released from the narrow bonds of ego and convention is enticing — and terrifying. (What we mean by *katharsis* has its roots in maenadic release.) Kerenyi understands how real this terror is: "In all human beings there lurks at all times an enemy of the god, ready to erupt and to murder him."[19]

To expose oneself to Dionysos always entails the danger of being taken over by this god who represents sacred energy at its most uncontained. Yet we may choose to risk this danger because we have had experiences that have taught us that at the very moment when we are taken away from ourselves as we ordinarily know ourselves, we may in some mysterious but profound way be brought in touch with ourselves. The ecstatic union with the god satisfies not only a longing for self-abandonment but also a deep hunger for an experience of ecstatic communion with all of life.

We need to remember that though intoxication may be Dionysos's hallmark, he is an *ecstatic* god of *fertility,* that the two are indissolubly, not accidentally, linked. The orgiastic rites associated with the worship of Dionysos are also still fertility rites, designed to evoke the fructifying powers of earth. Dionysos remains a son of the earth goddess. As Harrison puts it: "With Dionysos, god of trees and plants as well as human life, there came a 'return to nature,' a breaking of bonds and limitations and crystallizations," an escape from a strictly anthropomorphic religion.[20] As we have already noted, Dionysos opens us not only to the sacredness of the natural world, of the *zoe,* the life-force pulsing through vegetal and animal life, but to the sacredness of the natural in us, to the nature, we might say, in human nature. (Nature in Dionysos's realm is different from nature in Artemis's. The goddess represents the wilderness outside the city, the natural as the complementary correlate of the cultural; the god represents a wildness that threatens the city, that lurks within it as the never fully eradicable possibility of its dissolution.)

For Dionysos is the god of dissolution — and thus of wine, madness, sexual orgasm. The ecstasy that is the mark of the god's presence brings us in touch with who we are when all social constraints are removed, brings those who recognize him as a god into touch with their own potentially creative, transformative instinctual energy. In Dionysos's realm the point is sexual arousal, the experiencing of our own instinctual energy, an experience very different from the all-consuming other-directed passion that is Aphrodite's gift. In Aphrodite's realm we are taken over by a passion that only this one particular other in the whole world can satisfy, though he or she may be unavailable or forbidden or implacably inimical. In Dionysian passion there is no other — except the god, and he is no longer *other;* he and I are one.

Though I have experienced Dionysian passion taking me over, body and soul, in a way that challenges the very notion that one can distinguish body from soul, it remains true that my most powerful experiences of Dionysos have been mediated through the person of a lover who has appeared and disappeared and reappeared in my life for more than thirty years now. I love this man deeply and I grieve for him. He has been both votary of the god and the god's victim. When I first knew this man I saw him as allowing himself to be open to the god in a way that led me to hold my breath in awe and admiration and fear. I saw he was enlivened, not destroyed, and therefore became more ready to fully surrender myself to moments of passion when they came than I ever could have without his example. But as the years went on I saw my friend become more and more disenchanted with the world of everyday, more and more addicted to the escape ecstasy provides. I saw that the god now entered my friend not primarily through the naturally flowing juices of his own instinctual being here, his own *zoe,* but through the vine. Eventually alcohol so enslaved him that he had to choose between continuing to drink — and die — or to live without its support. He chose to live, and from time to time the god still showed himself in the seemingly inexhaustible love of life that this friend had always seemed to me to embody, but often the god was absent and I saw only an exhausted frame that brought me close to tears. And then my friend suffered a debilitating stroke. He almost died, but didn't. His body lives on, but the god seems to have gone for good. Or to be present in a different way.

For Dionysos, god of ecstasy, is also a god of death and of the underworld. Madness and underworld are in his realm closely connected, for both mean removal from the ordinary world of everyday reality. A fragment of Herakleitos affirms, "Hades is the same as Dionysos, the god to whom the mad orgies of the wild women are devoted." The rituals of Dionysos were celebrated at night and in the midst of winter. He was, again contrary to what the Greeks ordinarily meant by a god (that is, "an immortal"), a god who had died. The pertinent myth recounts that, though Dionysos was saved from death when his mother was killed, Hera sent the Titans after him when she learned of his birth from Zeus's thigh. They found the infant god, tore him to pieces, and began to eat him. Luckily Athene appeared in time to save his heart (or phallus), which she brought to Zeus, who swallowed it and eventually gave birth to Dionysos — again! Other indications of Dionysos's connection to the realm of death include the tale of Dionysos going to the underworld to rescue Semele, and the tale according to which Ariadne gave birth to him in the underworld. Dionysos is a god who suffered dismemberment and death — and who exposes us to a kind of dismemberment and death.

The dismemberment theme is important and should not

be subsumed under the death theme. For it is not only the Titans – or Zeus – who eat the god, but his followers as well. The maenads in their role as nurses of Dionysos suckled kids, but they also tore young goats apart and ate them – a communion rite in which the god offered his own body to the celebrants. We might also remember that Dionysos *is* wine; thus whenever libations of wine were offered to the other gods, it was the god himself who was being offered up.[21] This god dissolves the boundaries between the other gods and himself, between himself and us.

But as Kerenyi insists, despite the many deaths and dismemberments, Dionysos remains always indestructible *zoe;* he always escapes, always returns. "The realm of the dead opens, discharging Dionysos, that most living of all creatures."[22] In the rituals devoted to the god, men and women experienced Dionysos's living and dying in themselves, not just by becoming aware of the *analogy* between their lives and that of the vegetal cycle, but "in the most intimate life of their own sex," in the "high points of enhanced life" that sexual ecstasy provides *and* in "the sexual exhaustion that is so close to the exhaustion of *zoe.*"[23]

Under Dionysos's tutelage we experience how death is inherent *in* life, how (as Freud knew) Death and Eros are brothers. Through our sexuality we come to know ourselves as bodied creatures and thus sexuality prepares us to accept that as bodied beings we will die – and through our experience of the immortal god entering us at the moment of sexual possession we also discover the possibility of overcoming death; we learn as experiential reality, not just as idea of the indestructibility of life. Thus Dionysos represents a spirituality that is experienced in and through the body. As Harrison puts it, "The constant shift from physical to spiritual is the essence of the religion of Dionysos."[24]

Dionysos is the god who disappears and reappears, the god of death and life, as he is the god from whose rituals both tragedy and comedy derive. His festivals were celebrated in the winter and spring. It was said that when spring beckons the maenads try to waken the sleeping god; when it comes he reappears. In a sense this seasonal awakening is related to Dionysos being a god connected with the vegetal cycle, but that some of these rituals are celebrated only in alternate years is meant to make clear that the association with vegetal fertility is not the primary one. Dionysos is a god of souls, not just of the grain or even the vine. Thus the most important ritual observed in his honor, the Anestheria, though on the surface devoted to celebrating the new wine, was at a deeper level an all-souls festival, an occasion for the souls of the dead ("the thirsty ones") to emerge from the underworld and spend a day in our midst.

In the late classical world Dionysos was drawn into the orbit of the mystery religions and their promise of release from the fear of death. Though Mylonas may be right in his adamant insistence that Dionysos had no part in the Eleusinian mysteries, that he is not the Iacchos whose birth they celebrate, it is nonetheless true that the Greeks themselves and not just later scholars often identified Dionysos, Bacchus, Zagreus, Iacchos, and Bromios.[25] We should remember also that Dionysos is the god of the mask and that all these names are but masks. With the Olympian gods we sense an identity between the name and the god, but Dionysos is the unformed, unnamed reality behind the mask. So Mylonas may be too literal in saying that Dionysos had no place at Eleusis; he had none by that name.

Harrison claims that the Eleusinian mysteries (and, indeed, all of Greek religion) owe their spiritual depth to the appropriation of what the Greeks meant by the name Dionysos.[26] For she believes that the religion focused on the Olympian gods was too naive, too superficial, to help humans face the harsh realities of outward life or to help them deal with the fearful unconscious impulses that appear whether we invite them or not. Thus she sees Dionysos's reappearance in the classical world as a life-giving, life-deepening intrusion.[27]

Dionysos is *Lusios,* the loosener, a god who as many have recognized is especially appealing in times when the burdens of autonomy and responsibility, of existence in the social world, seem too constraining. But many have also discovered that "the spirit of Dionysos cannot be sustained for long without great danger. . . . We need the illusion of which Apollo is master, for illusion shields us from too much reality and enables us to go on living."[28] Nietzsche understood why Dionysos and Apollo belong together, why they are together at Delphi. Harrison believes that it was probably at Delphi that Dionysos was transformed into a god who could fit into the pantheon rather than destroy it.[29] Farnell notes that though Apollo had to seize Delphi from the Python violently, Dionysos was given his place there without a struggle. Indeed, "the brotherly union of the two Delphic divinities is so close that the personality of each is at certain points merged in that of the other."[30]

· 5 ·

Apollo

We turn to Apollo because in some sense Apollo and Dionysos do evoke each other; at first glance they seem diametrically opposed – the calm, rational Olympian and the emotionally labile intruder – but as their closeness at Delphi suggests, this is but a surface truth. Greek religion may, indeed, as Kerenyi claimed, be incomprehensible to us unless we understand the necessary if always ambiguous place of Dionysos within the pantheon;[1] but it is also true that it remains uncomprehended until we rightly grasp its perception of the relation between Dionysos and Apollo. We twentieth-century scholars have inherited the notion of Dionysos versus Apollo from the German Romantics (Bachofen, for example, said, "What is lacking in Dionysos will be found in Apollo") and from the early Nietzsche of *The Birth of Tragedy,* and many of us have found this antithesis useful as an allegorical representation of the conflict between what psychoanalysts call "id" and "ego," but it is not true to Greek religious history.[2] The two gods are, indeed, linked, but not so simplistically.

Still, most of us, I imagine, think first of Apollo as the god to whom Otto introduces us in his beautiful portrait: mysterious and unapproachable, calm and lofty, a god who comes from afar and withdraws for part of each year to a remote, mysterious place, the god who in the *Iliad* seeks to avoid the imbroglios among the gods and who puts an end to Achilles' rampage after Patroclos's death. "Apollo rejects whatever is too near – entanglement in things, the melting gaze, and equally, soulful merging, mystical inebriation and its ecstatic vision. He desires not soul but spirit." He directs our attention "to what transcends the personal, to the unchangeable, to the eternal forms."[3] Apollo represents clarity, coolness, objectivity, nothing in excess, the conscious, daylight view of things – though there is no real evidence that (at least until after the classical period) Apollo was ever seen as a sungod or confused with Helios. Apollo's "brightness" seems rather to refer to his radiant beauty or perhaps his purity.

Where Dionysos confuses gender distinctions, Apollo focuses on the importance of clearly defined boundaries, the gulf between the divine and the human, the difference between men and women. When Apollo says, "Know yourself," he means, "Know you are not a god; remember that though we are immortal, you are mortal." Where Dionysos is a god of women, Apollo seems to be a god of men. As Artemis is served almost entirely by female votaries, so her brother is attended by males. "The religion of Apollo appealed especially to the masculine temper, had little or no relation with the life of women, and — except in its prophetic ritual — rarely admitted female ministration."[4] Apollo is himself the idealized *kouros*, the youth on the edge of manhood at the height of his beauty, and preeminently the god of *kouroi,* who presides through his cult over their initiations into adult masculinity. He is a lover of youths who die — Hyakinthos, Cyparrisos — or at least die to being youths.[5] Robert Eisner observes how Apollo's homosexuality is really a sterile narcissism: in others he loves only his own traits.[6] He is a lover of women, too — among them, Hestia, Koronis, Daphne, Cassandra, the Sibyl, Sinope, Marpessa — but they, evidently not experiencing his love as love, refuse him as a lover.

Otto calls him the most Greek of all the Greek gods[7] — but recognizes that in the *Iliad* Homer puts Apollo on the side of Troy, as if to hint at the paradox that although he may seem to be the very embodiment of the Greek spirit, he is evidently not Greek in origin. Indeed, Apollo aids Paris in killing the archetypal Greek hero, Achilles. Thus to speak of Apollo as "the god who comes from afar" may be to say something more than that he rejects entanglement and ecstasy.

It is he, not Dionysos who has his origins outside of Greece, though there is disagreement among scholars as to whether Apollo comes to Greece from the far north or from Asia. Perhaps there were two origins as there are two cult centers, Delos and Delphi. Delos enters the tradition as Apollo's birthplace. According to the myth his mother Leto, after giving birth to the goddess Artemis, found her struggles were not yet over; Apollo was born only after nine further days of hard labor. Delos suggests an Eastern origin for the god as does the association with Leto and Artemis, both of whom are probably originally Asian goddesses — as does also Apollo's support of Troy.

At Delphi Apollo was recognized even in the mythical traditions as a latecomer, as a god who had come from afar, from the legendary land of the Hyperboreans. Ritual pillars, marking the stations along the god's way from the north, served as aniconic emblems of his presence. Farnell even suggests that perhaps the Delphic *omphalos* may have originated as such a pillar rather than as an icon of Gaia or the Python.[8] In Athens, where Apollo's cult never had close associations with those of Athene or Zeus, he was clearly viewed as a late-arriving god — though there was an attempt to establish him as having an ancient connection to Attica through the myth that made him the father of Ion, the eponymous founder of the city.

Thus Apollo, unlike many of the other gods, was never really tied to *a* place; he was a migrating god; his cult was a translocal one. When the Apollo oracle at Delphi came into prominence, it actively supported the colonizing activity of the Greek city states and played a major role in creating a Hellenized world.

Even though Apollo's association with Leto and Artemis is probably not original but rather an artefact of the superimposition of his cult on theirs, it may nonetheless suggest that like so many others of the gods he began as the son of a goddess. For, although according to the official genealogy Apollo is a son of Zeus, he never assumes the role that the son of the supreme god would be expected to have in a patriarchal system. All testimonies agree that vis-à-vis Zeus Apollo is subordinate to Athene; he is not accorded the rank or privilege due the favored heir. Apollo is at birth and remains Zeus's illegitimate son, the child of Leto, a second-generation Titaness through whom he is connected to the pre-Olympian world. At Delphi the cult group consists of Leto, Apollo, and Artemis (not Zeus) — a clearly matrilineal group: mother, brother, and sister. Apollo is a son of the matriarchy.

The emphasis in cult and myth on the closeness of the bond between Apollo and Artemis, brother and sister, says the same thing. Both Apollo and Artemis come from the same womb — and we might remember that the place name *Delphi* relates to a word that means "womb." Neither sister nor brother ever marries. This fits the assumptions of the matrilineal world where the sibling bond typically takes precedence over the conjugal; blood ties take precedence over legal ones. Indeed, in the Ionian settlements Artemis was often considered the supreme divinity and Apollo recognized only as playing the subordinate role of her priest.[9]

As an arriving, migrating god, Apollo was associated with the pastoral more than with the agricultural world, with Pan and the nymphs. We have already noted how in the "Hymn to Hermes" Apollo seeks to dissociate himself from this origin: to deed it to Hermes. But aboriginally Apollo seems to have had a different relation to the pastoral world from that attributed to Hermes. For Apollo was associated not so much with the gentle life of shepherds as with the forces that threaten them, the wolves. In myth wolves lead Leto to Delos, and her son is sometimes spoken of as "child of the she-wolf"; Apollo himself took on the form of a wolf when he seduced Cyrene. Farnell says it is probable that "the wolf was in some way regarded as 'the double' or the incarnation of the deity." Apollo may thus at first have been more a god of the bow and the hunt than of the flock, and Farnell cites evidence that early on his worship may have included rites of ecstatic possession that in the historical period one would expect only among the devotees of Dionysos.[10] Apollo's associations with Daphne and Hyakinthos and the plant imagery that pervades their cult suggest that when he came to Greece his cult was often superimposed upon already established vegetal chthonic cults.

Ever since I first read the published correspondence between Thomas Mann and Kerenyi, I have been interested in the dark (in the *Iliad* Apollo is spoken of as coming "like the night") and wolfish side of Apollo. In one of the first letters included in the collection the novelist thanks the classicist for introducing him to this Apollo — whom, he says, he immediately recognized.[11] The two agree that this hidden, shadow side of Apollo gives the god a spiritual depth that the purely "spiritual" version misses.

For the essence of Apollo, I have come to believe, is not purity but *purification.* We need to look again at the story of his arrival at Delphi. He comes, he murders the Python that guards the oracle on Gaia's behalf, and then he has to go off to be purified of the blood-guilt he has incurred. Later, enraged by their participation in the slaying of his son Asklepios, Apollo kills the Cyclopes and has to go off to be purified again, this time by putting himself in service to the mortal king Admetos. So it is likely that he was first worshiped as a purified murderer and only gradually — as an extension of what that signifies — became a god of law, justice, and order.[12]

Nilsson agrees that the most important thing about Apollo is that he provides purification to those polluted by blood-guilt. The rites of purification associated with Apollo were probably originally understood as offering an external ritualized cleansing but later led to a more moral, inward understanding of expiation.[13] Even Otto recognizes that Apollo may at first have been a terrible death-dealing god,[14] though like Apollo himself Otto would like to put that past aside as irrelevant to the figure the god has become, to emphasize the clarity, insight, concern for order and moderation of the later Apollo (which, he admits, is not yet very evident even in Homer's representation).

It may be strange at first to think of Apollo as a murderer, as a killer. But what is central here is the possibility of purification, the possibility (which the Oresteia celebrates) of putting an end to seemingly endless cycles of blood vengeance. Fully to understand the force of this means taking seriously the

Greek fear of the dead and their power to avenge, a fear given mythological representation in the dread Erinyes, the bloodthirsty ghosts of the murdered or otherwise grievously injured dead. For a god to have the power to free us from this fear is to be a god indeed.

Every nine years the Stepteria festival was celebrated at Delphi. The ritual involved a reenactment of the killing of the Python, Apollo's flight to Tempe in the far north for purification, and his return in triumph with the sacred laurel. Of course, there were other gods who offered purification: Zeus Meilichios healed Ixion, the first human murderer; Athene and Hermes purified the Danaides; the gods associated with the mysteries also purified. What distinguishes the purification provided by the Stepteria from most other such rituals is that those representing the polluter return "purified and rejoicing, bringing purification to their people." The violator himself becomes the one through whom the injured community has its purity restored. There was clearly an effort on the part of the priests of Delphi to gain supremacy over the rites of purification by establishing a more rational response to murder. Farnell sees the influence of Delphi as supporting the move toward a recognition of the distinction between justifiable and unjustifiable homicide and between inner purification and ritualistic purgation, whereas earlier understandings of the need for purification had been dominated by a fear of ghosts seeking vengeance whether or not they had been rightfully killed.[15]

The effort to encourage a reliance on the purification offered by Delphic Apollo largely succeeded, perhaps, Farnell suggests, because of how Apollo was imagined, perhaps "because the bright and genial character of Apollo, his antagonism to the shadowy powers of the chthonian world, was part of his aboriginal character"[16] (perhaps also because of Dionysos's association with Delphi and the growing importance of the cathartic deliverance his cult made available).

Apollo's role as purifier came to obscure his history as a killer. Thus when Apollo was invoked as a god of death, it was not because he was feared as a murderer but because he was welcomed as an expert marksman. Thus Apollo's bow is supplicated by those who hope for a gentle death, though only by men. (Artemis provides the same service to women.) Nor, despite his violent history, was Apollo viewed as a war god. In the *Iliad* he mostly keeps himself apart from the battle, though he is imagined as having played a part in those archetypal battles that the civilized Hellenes fought against such representatives of disorder and chaos as the Giants, the Centaurs, and the Amazons.

Apollo is also a god of plague and healing — in that order: a god who heals *because* he is a god who brings disease. Myth and rite express a homeopathic understanding of healing: the agent who brings the wound is the only one who has the power to effect its cure.[17] Because disease is pollution, healing and purification are seen as analogous. There are many tales about Apollo sending a plague upon a city and then eventually being persuaded to lift it. The beautiful remote Apollo temple at Bassae, for example, was built in gratitude for his bringing to an end a plague he himself had sent. Apollo is usually invoked as a healer of disasters affecting the whole community — war, drought, plague; his healer son, Asklepios, comes to be the god to whom individuals turn for help.

Among the most important festivals dedicated to Apollo was the Attic Thargelia, an ancient harvest ritual probably originally associated with an earth goddess.[18] The ritual, which involved the stoning of two *pharmakoi* (scapegoats), one woman and one man, was intended as effecting the annual purification of the city. The aim, as Harrison explains it, was not reform but expulsion. The ritual was not performed to appease a god, not as an act of atonement, but as riddance of pollution understood as posing a real physical threat of contagion. The *pharmakoi* were in all likelihood stoned to death, not as punishment or as an offering, but to make sure they were really gone. As Harrison puts it, the ritual was intended to assure a "really thorough housecleaning."[19] Farnell tells us how this ritual originated in response to the plague that infected Athens after the murder of Cretan Androgeos (the killing that led to the institution of the tribute of youths Attica had to send King Minos every year, the tribute that brought Theseus to Crete). He notes how when the ritual was first instituted the *pharmakoi* would undoubtedly have been understood as the representatives of the god, not as the god's enemies. This is changed when the ritual is no longer consciously understood, so that in the historical period the "ugliest," not the best, are chosen as victims.

Farnell is amazed at this proof of how strong "the bondage of ancient ritual" can be even when it is no longer understood and when it seems so incompatible with the later vision of a god "whom the higher imagination of the Greek so exalted and purified that death and bloodshed became unclean things in his sight."[20] The sense of that profound discrepancy leads Farnell to conclude: "We cannot find that such ritual, though it might attach itself to Apollo as an inheritance from an older or lower religious stratum, ever succeeded in marring the brightness of his character or clouding it with chthonian associations."[21] (The degree to which most scholars want to separate the "real" Apollo from this original more fearful side is striking; however, we can, of course, discern the beginnings of such idealization in the late classical world.)

Apollo is the leader of the muses and the father of Orpheus, god of the lyre, though the account in the "Hymn to Hermes" of Hermes inventing the lyre and then giving it to his elder brother suggests that it became associated with Apollo only after his arrival in Greece. Nonetheless, Olympian Apollo is the god of the arts, especially music. Nietzsche identified him with the formal, shaping aspect of art. Without disagreeing with this, I would emphasize Apollo's association with *harmony,* that is, once again with the subduing of chaos and conflict, as an event, as an accomplishment.

As a god of purification Apollo is the god of the fresh start. Thus it should not surprise us that though it is clear that he begins as a god attached to the matristic world, the world dominated by the goddess, he seeks to repress his origins and to overcome that world. Unlike Dionysos, who in a sense was always already there in Greece but nevertheless always remains a stranger, Apollo comes from far away but wants to out-Greek the Greeks, to shed his past, to overcome his connection to the pre-Olympian matriarchal world. Thus fully to comprehend the god we must look at his connection to the theme of *matricide*. He becomes the god of Delphi by killing the Python, who guarded the shrine on behalf of the earth mother Gaia whose oracle it had been since time immemorial. Apollo grants purification to two "matricidal protégés,"[22] Orestes and Alcmeon, who are pursued by the Erinyes on behalf of the earth mother (from whose perspective mother-killing is the most heinous and unforgivable of all crimes).

In his study of Greek sacred architecture Scully says: "Delphi must have seemed to the Greeks the place where the conflict between the old way, that of the goddess of the earth, and the new way, that of men and their Olympian order, was most violently manifest." He quotes the relevant lines from the *Eumenides:* Apollo "made man's ways cross the place of the ways of god / and blighted age-old distributions of power." We feel this at these sites — as, Scully has made me understand, we are meant to. When I read his description of how the pilgrim (in classical times and also now) first sees Apollo's temple from Athene's *tholos,* I remember my own most recent visit, when I decided I wanted to stay down below in the area dedicated to Athene Pronaia while my companion climbed up the Sacred Way to the god's temple. I remember so well feeling that I was sitting at the very navel of the earth, looking up at the beautiful columns thrusting up from earth against the open sky. Scully describes how as we make our way up the hill the city treasuries along the Sacred Way block our view of temple and valley, immerse us in the "jostle of human action." (How well I remember on another visit being so appalled by that bustling crowd that my companion and

I left the Way and spent an hour in the adjacent olive grove before proceeding to the temple!) As one makes one's way up the path the temple keeps appearing and disappearing, until as one makes the last turn one finally sees it standing proudly there against the open sky. Next to the temple itself in ancient times there stood a bronze palm tree, symbol of the goddess, symbol of the tree to which Leto held as in agony she gave birth to Apollo. And inside the temple at that time in its cavelike adyton was a stone omphalos, reminder of the pillar cult of the ancient goddess.

At Bassae, too (where the well-preserved temple makes the intended effect more available to present-day visitors), there is a dramatic contrast between what one experiences when one approaches the temple from outside and what one encounters within. The interior of this temple "explores to the full the double character of Apollo: its outward aspect, bright and Olympian, its inward aspect, chthonic and dark. . . . The emotions thus aroused must have made the complex nature of Apollo almost fully comprehensible."[23] This accords perfectly with my own experience at Bassae, a temple about which I remembered nothing when I so innocently came across a signpost directing me toward it while driving across Arcadia on my way from Olympia to Epidauros. When we had finally made our way up the steep and lonely path and stood before the temple, I said, *this* is Apollo!

Scully's words also describe perfectly my sense of Apollo, of what he represents that I recognize in myself. I see Apollo as signifying not (as he is often held to) the imperious self-sufficient ego, but rather the tensive co-presence of that in me which strives for command and clarity and the unsuppressable, lively turmoil with which it contends. We humans all suffer this conflict, the longing to assert autonomy and independence in the very face of our undeniable contingency and dependence. Yet I see why the Greeks imagined the bearing of this tension (not just one of its poles) through the figure of a male god. For it seems likely, as the feminist theorists influenced by the perspective of object relations suggest, that male children experience the need to separate from the mother and assert their independence of her more intensely than do female children.[24]

Not only at Delphi but throughout Greece the temples dedicated to Apollo were built in places where "the most awesome characteristics of the old goddess of the earth" were manifest, in the most remote, most tortuously approached, most imposing sites, where "the interior secrets of the earth" were most violently revealed. Scully suggests that we are intended to feel the conflict between the god's assertion of power manifest in the temple building and the goddess's earlier claim on the land. I remember feeling Gaia's power at Delphi on my first visit when I "knew" nothing of her once having been worshiped there. What I have learned from Scully is that the temple had been put just there so that I *would* recognize her presence *and* his, and the tension between them.

Thus Scully helps us see how Apollo's demand to us, "Know thyself, know you a human stand before the gods," strangely applies to the god himself. The Olympian stands before the ancient goddess of the earth, with his prideful claim to a power that is nonetheless puny compared to hers. Scully describes so well how lofty the temples appear as one looks from their heights to the valleys below, how amazed we are that they could be built where they are. They appear as arrogant intruders in sites recognized as holy long before the god's arrival. We cannot help but be impressed by the contrast between the abstract order of the human structure and the spectacular harsh wildness of the site. "Apollo is intellect, discipline purity. . . . Yet, he, too, cannot come to grips with the earth without being touched by it." Scully sees how these temples built "in the heart of a landscape haunted . . . by the images of the goddess and her power" are erected as almost flaunting challenges. But then from above, especially perhaps at Bassae, where a goddess temple sits at the very top of the peak high above the gods, Apollo's temple looks so small, so pure and yet so dwarfed — and then one understands the god's compulsion "to be far-shooting, death-bringing, full of threat."[25]

May Sarton's poem "At Delphi," captures a very similar sense of the impact of the tension between site and temple that alone communicates the full character of Apollo:

> *The site echoes*
> *Its own huge silences*
>
> *Wherever one stands,*
> *Whatever one sees —*
> *Narrow terror of the pass*
> *Or its amazing throat*
>
> .   .   .   .
>
> *Crags so fierce*
> *They nearly swallow*
> *A city of broken pillars.*
>
> .   .   .   .
>
> *I tell you the gods are still alive*
> *And they are not consoling.*[26]

Apollo not only takes over cult sites from the mother goddess, he also appropriates a "number of her native lovers," for instance, Hyakinthos, as his own.[27] Hyakinthos, originally the object of an ancient chthonic hero cult, was one of those dead heroes, sons of the mother, to whose grave people came as worshipers. His cult was absorbed by Apollo and so, as we noted in chapter one, at Amyclae the god's statue rests upon the hero's tomb. In myth he becomes Apollo's beloved whom the god inadvertently kills, the god's mortal double. Ovid retells the story in a way that convinces us of the depth of the god's grief at learning so painfully of the inescapability of the gulf that separates humans from the gods, mortals from the immortals. Fully to understand Apollo we must remember that he can weep, can be overcome with unassuageable regret, with unending grief.

Although most of the mortal women whom Apollo pur-

sued rejected him, a few responded willingly to his overtures,
including Chione, who happily made love to both Hermes and
Apollo on the same day, and Evadne, who secretly bore the
god's son in the fields (with the help of the midwife goddess
Eileithyia, whom Apollo had persuaded to come to her aid).
Not daring to bring the child home to her father, she left it in a
thicket where some snakes found and fed it. When the youth
grew up he went in search of his father, who granted him
the gift of prophecy. H.D. wrote a poem based on this story
which imagines Apollo as a gentle lover, their lovemaking as
like the brush of flower against flower:

> *I first tasted under Apollo's lips*
> *love and love sweetness,*
> *I Evadne;*
> *my hair is made of crisp violets*
> *or hyacinth which the wind combs back*
> *across some rock shelf;*
> *I Evadne*
> *was mate of the god of light.*
>
> *His hair was crisp to my mouth*
> *as the flower of the crocus,*
> *across my cheek,*
> *cool as the silver cress*
> *on Erotos bank;*
> *between my chin and throat*
> *his mouth slipped over and over.*
>
> *Still between my arm and shoulder,*
> *I feel the brush of his hair,*
> *and my hands keep the gold they took*
> *as they wandered over and over*
> *that great arm-full of yellow flowers.*[28]

This poem led me to wonder whether all those other females who saw Apollo as seeking to seize, to overpower, to
rape the women whom he desired might perhaps have found,

had they opened themselves to him, that he was not after all as undesirable a lover as they had assumed. A strange thought: perhaps Apollo like Dionysos is most destructive to those who seek to deny him! I don't even quite know what I mean by this but I am struck by how many tales there are of women who decide that, no matter what the cost, they would rather remain virgins than yield to the god. Were they right? Does Apollo truly represent an energy so profoundly alien to women that they must at all costs protect themselves against it? Or does he rather signify an energy that *might* destroy but that, if loved, could bring blessing?

Certainly there are many myths of women who reject the god: Hestia, who persuades Zeus to promise her that she may remain forever unwed rather than accept the suit of Apollo or Poseidon. Daphne, who flees the god and when she sees him gaining upon her transforms herself into a laurel bush. Sinope, who responded to the god's advances by requesting that he first grant her a boon; when he agreed, she asked that she might remain a virgin for the rest of her life. The Cumaean Sibyl, who asked that she might live as many years as there were grains in a pile of sand; Apollo said he'd only grant her the further boon of youth if she agreed to become his mistress, but she refused and lived to be a very wrinkled and gnarled thousand-year-old crone. And, most notable, the Trojan princess Cassandra, who happily accepted Apollo's granting her the gift of prophecy, but refused him as a lover; in retaliation the god, who could not take back his gift, announced that she would never be believed.

Jane Ellen Harrison sees Cassandra as originally a woman-prophetess of Gaia whom Apollo sought to take over as he took over the priestesses at Delphi. "Her frenzy against Apollo is more than the bitterness of maiden betrayed; it is the wrath of the prophetess of the old order discredited, despoiled by the new."[29] Harrison understands the myths that reveal how rarely Apollo succeeded in consummating his lust as masking a deeper truth: that Apollo is not really able to overpower the matrilineal world, to win free of his dependence on the goddess and her world. This becomes most evident at Delphi, the site that *seems* to represent Apollo's triumph over Gaia and all she represents. As Harrison observes: Apollo "took the name of the ancient Phoebe, daughter of earth, nay more he was forced, woman-hater, as he always was, to utter his oracles through the mouth of a raving woman-priestess, a Phoibas."[30]

At Delphi the prophets were always females (at first virgins, later postmenopausal women) whom the god entered with a frenzied possession that reminds us of the Maenads. Indeed, Rohde thinks the traditions about the Pythoness may well have been influenced by the Delphic absorption of Dionysian cultic elements,[31] though most scholars see the role played by these female intermediaries as simply an expression of Gaia's continuing influence: the source of the Pythoness's inspiration remains the subterranean world.[32] Or, perhaps, we might understand the Pythoness as the site of an ongoing struggle for her soul between the ancient goddess and the late-appearing god. For there is much in the symbolism of how the priestess receives her inspiration — she sits, feet spread apart on the tripod, and the god enters her from below — to suggest that Apollo takes sexual possession of her.[33] So whose priestess is she? Gaia's or Apollo's? The point may be precisely that the question remains open; Gaia and Apollo are still in contention.

H.D. has a poem in which she compares herself to the Delphic priestess:

> As the Pythoness stands by the altar,
> intense and may not move,
> till the fumes pass over;
> and may not falter or break,
> till the priest has caught the words
> that mar or make
> a deme or ravaged town;
>
> so I, though my knees tremble,
> my heart break,

> *must note the rumbling,*
> *heed only the shuddering*
> *down in the fissure beneath the rock*
> *of the temple floor;*
>
> *must wait and watch*
> *and may not turn or move,*
> *nor break from my trance to speak*
> *so slight, so sweet,*
> *so simple a word as love.*

The poem ends with her saying that "it was not chastity that made me cold" but fear, "fear that my weapon, tempered to a different heat," my "fiery-tempered, delicate, over-passionate steel" might be "over-matched" by that of the one she will not say she loves.[34] I understand the poem to be hinting of a deep hope that one might yield one's virginity and not be "over-matched." H.D. says this even more explicitly in her poem, "Delphi:"

> *now I know that the tale of his lust*
> *is lies*
>
> .   .   .   .   .
>
> *now I know*
> *that all who have spoken ill,*
> *who imperil*
> *and threaten the god,*
> *are holding their souls to a mirror.*[35]

Thus to malign Apollo is in some way to malign ourselves, to dishonor a part of us that is worthy of being honored as sacred but that is intrinsically, unavoidably in tension with another part of ourselves that we may *know* is somehow more primary. It is only as I keep in mind Apollo's dependence on the matrilineal world — which to be Apollo he *must* struggle against — that I know an Apollo whom I can welcome into our midst, into my life as a woman. But it seems signally important that I acknowledge the struggle for autonomy, for clarity, for objectivity as something I participate in, something I bless and love, but also something that I know can take over and separate me from other aspects of my being I also value.

I remember that as a God of oracles Apollo was spoken of as Apollo Loxias, Apollo the oblique. The responses his oracles give to human petitioners are indirect, veiled, ambivalent, often misleading, which is true of the god himself. From very early on part of what made Apollo Apollo was his association with the oracular. Farnell believes that Apollo was in a sense always a god of divination, well before his connection to Delphi.[36] Certainly he is connected with many other ecstatic oracles, though at these other sites the mediums are often male. They may drink of a sacred spring or inhale sacred vapors or interpret the sound of a running brook or the reflections in moving water; there seems to be no specifically Apollonian mode of divination.

Even Farnell, so convinced of Apollo's detachment from the chthonic, is not sure whether there were elements in his pre-Homeric character that led him to become a god who represents "aversion to the things of the lower world."[37] But as far back as we can clearly discern his presence, Apollo means, not ignorance of the underworld, but disengagement from it, not unstained purity, but purification, and a sustained commitment to represent *this* side of the divide, the day-lit rather than the dark underworld, the rational rather than the emotional, the "masculine" rather than the "feminine."

Thus there is much in which Apollo has no part: not only the sphere of the afterworld but also domestic life and with it the whole realm of women's lives and needs. Apollo is a god of public, political life, of what happens out in the open, in the external world. "He does not cross the threshold of the house, no part of inner domestic life is consecrated to him."[38] Nor is he engaged with the inner life. All "inner things" — the world within the earth, the world within the house, the world within the soul — are closed to him. His festivals are open public ceremonies; none occur at night or in the winter months. He has no connection with the mysteries, although his sons, Asklepios and Orpheus, play important roles in the later mystery cults.[39]

Apollo's sphere is, in a sense, a limited one, but he never claims to be the only god. At Delphi there was a ritual, celebrated shortly after his birthday, in which Apollo extends hospitality to the gods.[40] Delphi served as a mediator between humans and all the other gods, who except through the oracle gave no direct answer to human petitioners.[41] That is, in classical times it was felt that the only direct access one might have to any of the gods or goddesses was through Apollo. People came to Delphi to learn what god they had offended and what they must do to make up for their offense. The priests at Delphi thus came to be seen as involved with the right conduct of all rituals throughout the Greek-speaking world.

And, most especially, as we have already noted, at Delphi Apollo welcomed Dionysos to share his cult. In the *Eumenides* the Pythia gives first honor, in the prayer which opens the play, to Earth and then to Apollo and to Athene Pronaia, but she also acknowledges "Bromios, whom I forget not, sways this place." We need to remember this: that Dionysos was *welcomed* at Delphi. As Scully puts it: "The depth of Greek religious experience brought Apollo, by the late archaic period, to share his shrine with Dionysos." From above, from the perspective of Dionysos's theater, which moves in rhythm with the shape of the hillside within which it sits, Apollo's temple no longer seems in strife with its setting. The site now seems sheltering.[42] It is as though for all his contending with her, as to be Apollo he *must* contend, the goddess nevertheless embraces him.

· 6 ·

Hephaistos and Ares

Why Apollo became an Olympian, one of the Twelve, is obvious; it is less evident with respect to his two half-brothers, Hephaistos and Ares, the legitimate sons of Zeus, the children of his marriage with Hera (though there are traditions according to which Hephaistos was not fathered by Zeus but was rather the parthenogenetically conceived child of Hera). These two brothers are radically different from one another, one effete, the other hypermasculine, but perhaps just because of that they seem to belong together in a *coniunctio oppositorum*. Certainly over and over again they keep appearing as two players in the same stories, and the theme that keeps reappearing with respect to both is *rejection*.

Neither has much connection to the natural world. Sons of a deity who is himself primarily viewed as anthropomorphic, Hephaistos and Ares represent aspects of *human* nature, disassociated aspects, human creativity, human aggression.

Although Hephaistos is often thought of as originally a god of fire, it is not at all likely that he really begins as such. Whereas *Gaia* is the common noun used to speak of the earth that our feet tread and our plows break and *Hestia* the common noun used of the hearth fire, *Hephaistos* was never anything but a proper noun, the name of the god.[1] Nor was Hephaistos ever associated with celestial fire, with the lightning bolts that belong to father Zeus and were fashioned for him, not by his blacksmith son, but by the Cyclopes. No, Hephaistos is the god of terrestrial fire, volcanoes, and, even more importantly, the fire of the smithy. And it is probably more accurate to think of him as the firesmith than as the fire, as the alchemist, the artist. He appears in myth mostly as the fashioner of exquisitely beautiful, intricately designed works of art: beautiful jewelry for the Titaness Thetis, who raised him after he had been discarded by his mother,

Athene's weapons, Achilles' armor, the sickle with which Perseus decapitated Medusa, Harmonia's necklace, Hera's golden throne, Aphrodite's golden girdle, palaces for each of the gods.

He is not a god of the heavens, nor is he a god of the underworld. His association with volcanoes is relatively late, probably derived from his association with metallurgy rather than the other way about, and more important in the Roman than the Greek period. He has no connection with the mysteries nor any cult association with the divinities who play a prominent role in them.

He is a human culture hero, *homo faber,* writ large: the artist as divine. (Many scholars, Gerda Lerner among them, have suggested that it is the beginning of the Bronze Age, the discovery of metalworking, of tools and weapons, that marks the beginning of the move from mother-worshiping cultures to patriarchal religion and culture.[2] Thus we might view Hephaistos as the god whose appearance marks this transition.) In the Homeric "Hymn to Hephaistos" he is greeted as the god who taught men to work. Men "who formerly lived in caves in the mountains like animals," now, thanks to Hephaistos's famous skill, know how to work so that their lives are easy the whole year long.[3]

Yet he is an ancient god, and even, in one tradition, a child of Cronos.[4] His mythic and cultic associations with Athene and Ericthonios suggest that he was worshiped in Attica well before the arrival of the Ionians. Probably in that early period when metalworking seemed a magic art, epitomizing sacred transformative power, Hephaistos was recognized as a truly important god. Hephaistos works *with* the natural elements, as Apollo works *against* them. He is, indeed, always a reconciling, harmonizing god, always running back and forth between his parents trying to smooth over differences, to act as a peacemaker, trying, as Philip Morton suggests, somehow to reconcile the patriarchal and matriarchal archetypes.[5]

But in the classical period, when all work of the hands was denigrated, associated with the status of slave not noble,

Hephaistos's rank among the gods declined.[6] As Murray Stein notes, Hephaistos is "the only Olympian god who works."[7]

Although Hephaistos was deemed an Olympian, he was imagined as spending all of his time on earth, where he had been thrown by one or the other of his rejecting parents, depending on which story you prefer, though, of course, in the way of myths, both are true. According to one version, Hera conceived Hephaistos parthenogenetically because of her jealousy at Zeus's parthenogenetic birthing of Athene. But when the child was born, its feet were turned front to back, and in disgust Hera threw him out of heaven. The other story relates that Zeus threw him down from Olympos in anger at Hephaistos's taking his mother's side in a quarrel between the parents; the god's foot was broken as he landed on the island of Lemnos and he remained lame forever after.

In both accounts he is rejected and crippled: in one rejected because crippled; in the other crippled because rejected. (Farnell reminds us that many fire gods are imagined as crippled — Vedic Agni for instance is footless — perhaps in analogy to weak, wavering flames.[8]) Among the Olympians, only Hephaistos was not imagined as physically perfect, divinely beautiful. There is much in the tales about Hephaistos to suggest that he was imagined as making beautiful things to compensate for his own ugliness.

That in some traditions Hephaistos has no father suggests that the Greeks imagined him as somehow deficient in masculinity. He is the gentle, introverted, intuitive artist, the peacemaking son, the male trying to be a woman. Hephaistos was rescued from drowning when Hera threw him into the sea by the sea goddess Thetis (representative of a more ancient strata of the goddess world than Olympian Hera.[9]) Thetis raised him for nine years in a "secret place" where he acquired his artistic gifts. Thus his creativity is in some way learned from the goddess, from his sojourn in her space, a second, more welcoming womb (which is just how Jungian theory would encourage us to imagine an artist's development: in *Symbols of Transformation* Jung speaks of our longing to return to the mother's womb – which he claims Freud understood only in literal incestuous terms – as a longing for contact with the creative unconscious[10]).

Another myth relates that after he had perfected his artistic skills, Hephaistos, in retaliation for his mother's rejection of him, sent her an elaborately worked beautiful golden throne. When the goddess sat upon this magical chair, she discovered that it bound her fast, suspended upside-down in midair. Then when the gods called upon Hephaistos to release his mother, he refused, claiming to have no mother. (Eventually, of course, he was persuaded to relent.) This suggests that Hephaistos may want to usurp her power, claim it as his own.

As wounded male, Hephaistos may feel he knows what it is like not to be dominant, and that therefore he can be just as sensitive or intuitive as any woman. But, although he has an artist's intuitive sense of form he seems to have no intuitive sense of others, and especially not of women; he completely misunderstands their response to him. The many myths about his involvements with female deities other than Thetis all show him being rejected. His mother rejected him at birth. According to Homer Hephaistos was married to Aphrodite, but to be married to the goddess of love is almost by definition to be cuckolded, as Hephaistos was by his brother Ares. After learning of this adulterous liaison Hephaistos sought to embarrass his wife and her lover by devising a golden net that would chain them to the bed as they began their vigorous lovemaking. He thus hoped to put them in a situation where he could display their shame to all the other gods. But the gods only laughed, and their laughter was directed not so much at the adulterous pair as at the deceived husband.

It is said that Hephaistos came to Zeus's aid when the father of the gods was having the massive headache that was his equivalent of labor pains. Hephaistos opened up his forehead with an axe so that the goddess Athene might come forth, already full grown, already uttering her awesome battle cry. Here he seems to play the role of a male midwife. Later Hephaistos sought to make love to Athene. Though she spurned him, he was so aroused that he ejaculated on her thigh. Disdainfully, she rubbed off the semen, which spilled onto the earth and impregnated Gaia (who later gave birth to Ericthonios, the father of the Athenians).

Hephaistos fashions the first human female, Pandora, in what Stein interprets as a mimicking of female creativity, thereby suggesting that perhaps all Hephaistos's artistic activity could be understood in the same way. Pandora can be seen as "a representative of the all-giving Mother herself, which has been scaled down to human size through the arts of Hephaistos."[11]

Thus Hephaistos can be understood to represent the inherently crippled (because arising out of a resented lack) but beautiful male attempt to simulate female procreativity. As Stein puts it: "The forge of Hephaistos is therefore the birthplace of spirit," of artistic cultural creativity as a sublimation of male envy of female biological generativity.[12]

I have been struck by how many of the men I have known well and deeply loved have identified with this god, even though I have seen them primarily in other ways, in relation to Hermes or Dionysos or Apollo. These men, in moments of tenderness, have spoken of how their deepest inner sense of themselves includes a sense of a primary incurable woundedness, an irremediable crippledness, which they usually succeed in hiding but which is nonetheless always there. Often they see this as somehow related to a sense of having been rejected by their mothers from very early on. They feel haunted by the never-quenched hope of somehow winning back her love, by being good enough, sweet enough to endear themselves to her. They become placators, like Hephaistos himself. Unlike the hero son who feels his mother expects from him the glory won through audacious deed or mighty accomplishment, these men want to bring her (or her surrogates) something they have made that is so compellingly beautiful that she will at last in gratitude offer them her withheld blessing. In a sense they are active; they make beautiful things, give in generous ways, but they also manifest a kind of passivity, for they want to be appreciated, be loved, to receive. They feel themselves always to be still waiting for the blessing.

Strange, though, how often when they speak of this it is as though they forget that Hephaistos, despite *and because of* his deformity, was recognized as a *god*, as representing a sacred mode of energy. Hephaistos works with his hands, with his body, that misshapen body. Culture-making in his realm is not simply an intellectual or spiritual endeavor; it represents not a rising above the material realm but a working with it. In the figure of Hephaistos the Greeks celebrated as divine that first step beyond immersion in the natural world when we humans discover our capacity to transform the given — and to do so not simply for utilitarian purposes, for biological survival, but for the sake of beauty. Hephaistos does not, like Hermes, just *discover* the luck already inherent in an apparently unfortunate turn of events; he is an alchemist who *transforms* the ugly into the beautiful, lead into gold. And, of course, this has to be true of Hephaistos himself. The beauty I find so evident in these men I love is not a hidden inner beauty, always already there, but a beauty achieved through the work of transformation. The work shows; as in a work of art the *work* that lies behind it is part of what makes it beautiful.

In *The Goddess* I suggested that from the female perspective Hephaistos might also represent women's wounded, silenced artistic creativity.[13] Hera's rejection of her son might be understood as a rejection of playing the role of being the mother of sons who get to create while she as a woman remains consigned to the role of procreator (and in reaction may feel tempted to dismiss creative activity as simply a pitiable substitute procreativity). We women need to reclaim Hephaistean energy as part of our own being. The gift of culture-making, of transformative activity, is not just a male prerogative but rather an integral aspect of being human, and as such both curse and blessing. It may, indeed, always proceed from a sense of need and inadequacy. But then, acknowledging need, acknowledging finitude, and going on to

live as beautifully as we can manage may be *the* challenge of our human being here. The Greeks understood that it may take a god to teach us this simple truth.

◆

Although there are no cult connections between Hephaistos and Ares, Ares appears in many of the same myths as does Hephaistos. Both are children of Zeus and Hera; each is sometimes said to have been parented only by Hera. Hephaistos catches Ares in bed with Aphrodite. Ares is sent to persuade Hephaistos to unbind Hera from the throne on which she sits suspended in midair but fails. (Dionysos succeeds by getting Hephaistos drunk!) And Ares, like Hephaistos, is rejected by Athene, though in his case not as a lover but as a warrior: "Be not afraid of violent Ares," the goddess tells Diomedes on the Trojan battlefield, "that thing of fury, evil-wrought, that double-faced liar."[14]

Again like his brother, Ares is rejected by Zeus, who in the *Iliad* tells him, "To me you are most hateful of all gods who hold Olympos." Though Zeus never literally throws Ares down from Olympos, on this same occasion he goes on to say that if Ares weren't his own son he would send him down to the deepest depths of Tartarus among the Titans where he by character belongs.

> *Were you born of some other god and proved so ruinous*
> *long since you would have been dropped beneath the gods of the bright sky.*[15]

The theme of Ares' isolation among the gods is echoed in *Oedipus Rex,* where the chorus summons Dionysos to drive Ares, "the god unhonored among the gods divine,"[16] from Thebes. And on the east frieze of the Parthenon Ares is placed among the gods, but alone.[17]

As Harrison puts it, Ares *is* a god but unhonored by his fellow gods. He is the god of war — and nothing else. Neither cult nor myth gives any hint of a wider function or a more complex character. He is the god of brute battle rage, of slaughter, unlike Athene, the goddess of the civilized art of war. The Greeks saw him as an anachronistic reminder of their own barbaric past and yet they knew that the passion to do battle *is* a sacred energy that can take hold of us and push aside all else. (Having watched during the recent war with Iraq how easily war passion can still seize hold of us Americans and reading the newspapers week by week and seeing this energy so easily summoned forth all over the world, I have no doubt of the power of this archetype.) We need to remember that for an energy to be recognized as divine, for it to be embodied in a god, does not mean that it is a beneficent energy.

Ares seems never to have been the primary deity of any Hellenic group; he may originally have been the war god of a submerged people, a god who was made to carry an energy that could not be denied but could be disowned. Jean Bolen aptly calls him "patriarchy's shadow."[18] It would also be easy to see him as a conventional animus figure, assertiveness and courage transmuted into aggressiveness and hubristic bravado. Not surprisingly, in the *Iliad* he is represented as siding with the Trojans.

As god of war, Ares is sometimes seen as associated with all violent death. Indeed, he once had to stand trial as a murderer, though the Olympian court acquitted him on the grounds of justifiable homicide. (He killed a son of Poseidon who was trying to rape Alcippe, one of Ares' own daughters.) But Ares plays no part in Greek funeral rites, has no association with underworld deities; from his perspective there is no soul meaning attached to death, only the end of physical life. Nor is Ares (unlike Poseidon) connected to the stormy violence of the natural world.

Though a war god, he is not effective on the battle field. Poseidon's twin sons, Otus and Ephialtes, once captured Ares and then stuffed him into a bronze jar where he stayed for thirteen months until rescued by Hermes. During the Trojan War Ares is wounded by Herakles and Diomedes, and later Athene knocks him flat, despite Aphrodite's rather laughable attempt to come to the aid of her paramour.

Thus he was never seen by the Greeks as epitomizing the ideal hero, nor are the heroes represented as calling upon him for support on the battlefield. Ares seems to a hypermasculine figure, an ugly, destructive caricature of what manhood signifies. He makes us think of warrior cults where it may have been important to exaggerate the difference of men from children and women, where manhood was earned through undergoing a series of ordeals. Ares' brutality seems the correlate of having to carry the aggression of others (of Hera, of women more generally?). The burden of carrying such projections might naturally lead to an anxiety about phallic potency and a consequent swaggering exaggeration of it. All engagements come to be understood in zero-sum terms: one is either victor or victim. Ares is "the wild man" (to use Bly's term) who has not yet learned to acknowledge the pain of his rejection by his father. Because he cannot acknowledge his own woundedness, he can only inflict wounds on others.[19] If we say Hephaistos mimics the mother, perhaps we might also say Ares mimics the father, hides behind a false, artificial potency.

And yet, and yet... I keep remembering that Aphrodite

loved this violent god. Aphrodite, who loved only where she chose to love, turned to him more than to any other lover. She bore him four children. Two of them may represent the less attractive sides of Ares – Deimos, fear, and Phobos, panic. But the other two are Eros, god of love, and Harmonia, their only daughter. (She married Cadmus of Thebes, the king who had to serve Ares for eight years in punishment for killing a snake guarding a spring sacred to the war god. Their children include Dionysos's mother, Semele.) Indeed, it may be the cultic association of Ares and Aphrodite at Thebes that gave rise to their association in myth. Aphrodite loved Ares (as I believe that Persephone came to love Hades). Fully to understand the god means trying to understand her love. Perhaps the goddess saw something attractive about him that others had missed or, more likely, paired with her he is attractive in a way that separated from her he cannot be. I imagine them both feeling that their instinctual passionate nature has met its match and delighting in that. (Aphrodite was furious when she learned that Ares was having an affair behind her back with Eos – and punished the nymph by causing her to fall hopelessly in love with one beautiful man after another.) Because Aphrodite can bless Ares' passion, she transforms it. They are able to celebrate "the battle of the sexes" as a battle both can win.

Ares was involved in many other liaisons and bore many sons, most of whom were violent men. But, surprisingly, there are no accounts of his forcing himself upon women as there are of so many others among the gods. I note also that Ares was the god of the Amazons and father to their queen, Penthesiliea. The Amazons were women in whom Ares' war rage was directed against men – though they were more effective warriors than he. Again, there seems to be a hint here that when appropriated by women this Ares energy could be directed in creative ways. Although at some temples dedicated to Ares, women were forbidden admittance, in Tegea and perhaps elsewhere as well there was a sacrificial feast to Ares from which men were excluded,[20] as though perhaps women had access to a secret side of the god.

When reading Seltman's account of Ares I suddenly understood how differently we might relate to Ares if we saw
him not as unlovable but as unloved, as unlovable because
unloved, rather than the other way around.[21]

As I reflect on how both Ares and Hephaistos are imagined
as rejected gods, I think of them as representing energies we
reject in ourselves (and here I am thinking primarily of us
women). How often we separate out both creativity and aggressivity as male energies. We tend to think of Hephaistos
and Ares as at work only in men, as representing what we
pity in men or what we most actively resent. But, strangely,
that very pity and resentment are signs of Hephaistos and
Ares at work *in us.* Our sympathy for the sense of inadequacy that underlies male creative activity may make us too
compliant, too indulgent, too self-abnegating. Our anger at
patriarchal domination of women may make us angry, hostile
women. Projection of these energies onto men, denying that
we too are pulled to world-making and we too experience the
longing to dominate and subordinate, such projection represents precisely the separating out of these energies from
the equally powerful longings to bless things as they are, to
at times be ruled over rather than always in charge, which
makes the energies represented by Hephaistos and Ares seem
destructive.

Perhaps we should recall that though both gods experienced rejection from many directions, Thetis knew how to
welcome Hephaistos with love, as Aphrodite did Ares.

· 7 ·

Poseidon

T hough Ares and Hephaistos may seem like relatively minor gods, I am aware of having a strong connection to them. Among the Olympians it is Poseidon whom I know least well. Indeed, when I first began reflecting on the gods I simply left him out and didn't even notice I had done so until a friend pointed it out — much as in writing *The Goddess* I had left out Hestia, quite unconsciously. Hestia later came into clear focus for me;[1] Poseidon has not yet done so.

And yet one of my favorite places in all of Greece is his temple at Sounion. I have never seen it from the sea, never glimpsed its pure profile against the blue Greek sky, never directly experienced it as "the true landfall after the treacherous Aegean, the sign of home and victory."[2] But I know what it is to stand leaning against one of the temple's columns looking out at the bounded seaview and the many islands visible in the distance, what it is like to stand on the edge of the seacliff, alone with the sea. Always when I come, I stay until long after sunset, stay until all others have gone.

Always I feel I know why they built the temple there, always I feel the god's presence. But somehow the cult history, the myths, the attributes don't touch me as the temple does. It communicates that a god is here; they somehow do not. It is as though for me he is a submerged god, submerged first by the goddess, then by Zeus.

Poseidon was probably brought to Greece around 2000 B.C.E. by an Indo-European group known as the Minyans. He was their version of the sky god, their Zeus. The Minyans came with the horse, the wheel, and Poseidon. His name, *Poteidan,* means "the potent husband of earth" and from early on he was paired with *Da-Mater,* earth mother. Thus Poseidon exists in language only as husband. His most familiar title is *Ennosigaios,* Earth-Shaker, which, as Kerenyi says, suggests an image of the god as a "violent copulator."[3] He comes to Greece from outside, but he is absorbed into the indigenous earth goddess religion, not as son but as husband.

Originally, as a god of the invaders he was, of course, not a god of the sea (since there was no sea in the northland from which he had come), though he may always have been associated with water, perhaps with the rain, more likely with the fertilizing stream of freshwater rivers.

From early on Poseidon seems to have been closely associated with horses. The fruit of his liaison with Medusa was the winged horse Pegasus (and he was also father to Bellerophon, the hero who eventually tamed the magic steed). Although Poseidon was not related to the Centaurs (human-headed creatures with the bodies of horses), he aided them in their flight from Herakles.

As Poseidon was absorbed into the established goddess cult, he came to be identified with the bull, ancient symbol of her consort in Crete and in the Greek myth cycles involving Crete. Thus it was Poseidon who caused Pasiphae to fall in love with the bull that her husband, King Minos, had failed to offer in sacrifice, and it was Poseidon who sent the bull that caused Hippolytos's death. (I know that much of my own sense of Poseidon derives not directly from my childhood or adult reading of Greek mythology, but from what I learned in the years between from reading Mary Renault's *Bull from the Sea*.)

Later, when the Zeus-worshiping Achaeans came into Greece around 1300 B.C.E., Poseidon was absorbed into the Zeus religion as an older (in Hesiod) or younger (in Homer) but always subordinate brother. Otto says that it is clear that for Homer Poseidon's true greatness belongs to the past, that the poet depicts him as a god representative of a now almost anachronistic form of divine energy.[4]

In myth Poseidon becomes another son of Cronos, who, like Hades, was swallowed by his father immediately after birth, or perhaps thrown into the sea, or maybe raised secretly by a mother who tricked her husband into swallowing a horse in place of the child god. Despite the appearance of swallowing in the mythologem, Farnell is certain that Poseidon never has any contact with the cult of the dead, with any chthonian rites.[5] Thus Poseidon is easily distinguished from Hades, albeit not from Zeus.

In the later mythology Olympian Poseidon is linked with Olympian Demeter, as their names may have made inevitable. He falls in love with her; she seeks to evade his embrace by turning into a mare; he becomes a stallion and mounts her. Their children are the horse Arion and Despoina, a goddess of the underworld very like Persephone. In this tale as in several others it is difficult to distinguish clearly between Poseidon and his more powerful brother. (Tripp even mentions a tradition according to which Poseidon fathers Athene![6]) In Homer Zeus is at one point even given control over the sea, and in visual representations he is sometimes shown as a rain god with wet hair. Indeed, in the art of the classical period it becomes nearly impossible to tell Zeus and Poseidon apart, unless Poseidon's trident is represented in such a way that it is clearly not a scepter or a thunderbolt — though sometimes in later Hellenistic depictions Poseidon is shown in the more wild, stormy, melancholic poses felt befitting a poetic conception of a god of the sea.[7]

Even Homer seems to have imagined Poseidon as more physical, more violent than Zeus, more clearly still tied to the natural world. Certainly in the epic tradition Poseidon was associated with earthquakes and tidal waves, with nature at its most violent and frightening. But Poseidon is not simply an "ancient god of nature's violence"; he is also a god representative of the human command over the natural world, a god not just of horse and sea but of the horsetamer and the sailor, as Apollo is god of both plague and healing. Poseidon is associated with "actions that demand the consent of nonhuman forces," as long ago he was the husband, not the victim, of the earth goddess.[8]

Once absorbed into the Olympian cult, Poseidon becomes a sea god. Scully believes it is obvious why a horse god should also be a god of the sea; he invites us to picture Poseidon leaping above the ocean's breakers like a rearing stallion.[9] The mythological version of how Poseidon came to rule over the sea is that after Cronos had been overthrown, his three sons divide the world between them and by lot Poseidon receives dominion over the sea. Or, according to another tale, he gains this kingdom by marrying Amphitrite, daughter of Nereus or Oceanos (both Titanic sea gods).

Like earlier sea divinities, preeminently Proteus, Poseidon was a shape-changer. (Proteus is sometimes said to be a son of Poseidon, but was probably a much more ancient god of the sea, perhaps displaced by Poseidon as the Olympian religion gained dominance. The most familiar tale about Proteus, a god gifted with foreknowledge, describes him transforming himself into one animal after another so as to elude being "pinned down" by Menelaus and having to tell Menelaus what he must do to make his way safely home from Troy.) Poseidon, on the other hand, changes shape not to elude capture but to secure his prey. Thus it is said that he raped Demeter as a horse, Medusa as a bird, others as a ram, a bull, a dolphin.

Often Poseidon appears in mythology as a loser, who nevertheless does not completely disappear. (Perhaps there are no ultimate defeats in the struggles among the gods; in the long run each must be given his due.) According to some traditions Poseidon had a place at Delphi alongside Gaia before Apollo arrived, but Apollo managed to get him to give up his claim to the oracle.[10] Poseidon's rivalry with Zeus at one time led him to join Hera and Athene in a revolt against "the father of gods and men." They managed to tie the god up, but when Thetis threatened to send one of the Hundred-handed to Zeus's aid, the alliance was quickly ended. Poseidon finds himself contesting Hera for dominion of the Argive cult but loses. He and Athene compete as to which is to be the major deity of Attica; she wins. Poseidon proposes to Hestia but is refused; he drops his rivalry with Zeus for the favor of Thetis as soon as he learns that she is destined to have a son who would overcome his father. There are traditions that Poseidon also unsuccessfully wooed both Hera and Artemis.

In his relations with women Poseidon is often represented as a ravisher. Included among women whom he seduced are two of the Pleiades and innumerable Nereids and nymphs. He takes the beautiful maiden Caenis against her will, but then in repentance agrees to grant her wish that she might be turned into a man and never again have to suffer such violation. Some say Poseidon was the sea-monster whose wrath the sacrifice of Andromeda was intended to placate, though luckily Perseus came to her rescue before she was killed. Poseidon rapes Demeter and Medusa and manages to sleep with Theseus's mother on the night of this Troezen princess's wedding to the king of Athens. There is, however, some ambiguity attached to these tales; it is not always clear how seriously the women resisted the god.

And we know there must be another side: the mother of the violent, cruel giants, Otus and Ephialtes, falls in love with Poseidon and conceives her sons by pouring seawater into her lap; she, not he, does the seducing in this tale. And women administered Poseidon's cult at both Thebes and Troezen.

Poseidon's children include the Homeric Cyclopes (a different group from the Cyclopes born of Gaia, who fashioned Zeus's thunderbolts), Polyphemos and his brothers, one-eyed, raw-meat-eating giants who recognized neither the gods nor their laws. He also fathered the aforementioned twins, Otus and Ephialtes, and many other brutish bandits. But among Poseidon's offspring are also the beautiful winged horse Pegasus (who has so often been regarded by poets as figuring their own flights of fancy) and the warrior Chrysaor, several of the Argonauts, the giant hunter Orion, and, most importantly, the hero Theseus, to whose aid Poseidon came at almost every turn of this long-lived hero's life. The only daughter I recall is Despoina, the Persephonelike figure to whom Demeter gives birth after lying with Poseidon.

Poseidon's relation with the beautiful youth Pelops was more tender than any of his involvements with females.

Though their intimacy was short-lived, both remembered it as a blessed interval, and when it came time for Pelops to seek a bride, the god happily came to his support.[11]

I wonder if men have a clearer access to Poseidon's tender side. I wonder if I don't "get" Poseidon because I don't "get" anger, because I'm afraid of it, submerge my own and fear being flooded by another's. I wonder if it's really Poseidon I experience at Sounion — or Aphrodite, the ancient goddess of the halcyon sea.

· 8 ·

Zeus

When we women come to consider Zeus, all our feelings about male gods, fathers, men, patriarchy are likely to be stirred up. Just as I don't know Poseidon well enough, I may know Zeus too well, or rather may see him in a more forgiving light than many other women will. For I am a father's daughter, and I identify Zeus with the encouraging inner voice of the father, though I know full well that for others that voice has been a stifling, critical, judgmental one. I also know that Zeus has many voices, many faces, many names, as he has many mistresses and many children. There is no possibility of doing justice to his multifacetedness. Each of us can only name the Zeus she sees, and what I see is primarily the god who accepts and blesses the rich diversity and complexity of things as they are: the Zeus who presides over a polytheistic world.

Although it is customary to say that Zeus comes to Greece with the Achaeans around 1300 B.C.E., there is another sense in which we can't really say from *where* he comes: the Aryan world, Dodona, Crete, Arcadia. Certainly from a time soon after his supposed arrival in Greece his cult was common to all the Hellenic tribes. To express the sense that he belongs to all Greeks, indeed, that to be Greek means to honor Zeus as chief among the gods, in the classical world he came to be known as Zeus Panhellionos.

Kerenyi says that "the beginning of Greek religion is the name Zeus."[1] The Aryans brought the name, which is the equivalent of *theos,* to Greece. *Theos* originally refers, Kerenyi tells us, to an event, the moment of lighting up, the experience of being confronted by a god, to wit, *epiphany.* The word also suggests a new time in contrast to an old, a quality of newness. The number of events that could be *theos* was always infinite.[2] Thus what the Greeks meant by Zeus was the

experience of light appearing, of the sacred as event, of overwhelming divine energy. To say "Zeus" meant "the god is *here*,
the god has just arrived in this moment." Zeus is not so much
the bright sky or the sun or the stars as radiance, luminosity,
the event of day beginning to dawn, the flash of lightning, the
thunderbolt. (Though later tradition has it that the thunderbolts were not originally his, that during his struggle with the
Titans, the more ancient gods, Zeus received them from the
Cyclopes whom he had released from imprisonment in Tartarus.) Zeus is also places struck by lightning, meteors, and
mountaintops. He was worshiped at mountain shrines, and in
truth he was a mountain god to begin with. Zeus is identified
with Mt. Olympos, which is not so much a particular mountain in a particular locality as the highest mountain of all. Only
later is Zeus imagined primarily anthropomorphically; at first
the mountain is itself regarded as the most telling symbol of
his presence.

Zeus's first appearance in Greece was at Dodona. As H.D.'s
poem "Dodona" attests, the "lighting up" that was experienced there was not a flash of lightning in the physical sky
but insight, the revelation given by the oracle.[3]

You have taken away the terror from the sun,
you have given new light to the day.
. . . .
we come from afar,
we await, we implore, we hide and attend,
we are lost,
without friend, loving your word the more;

we fear while we wait,
will you speak,
will you heal?
shall we creep,
shall we kneel?
shall we stand
with palms spread?

shall we bring white or red wine,
shall we bake brown or white bread?[4]

Some say Zeus came to Dodona with the goddess Dione (her name means simply "goddess"; it is a feminine form of his own) and left her there to preside over the oracle on his behalf. Others say that she was already there, that he married the goddess of the oracle. This seems likely: at Dodona he was called "the husband of Dione," as he was almost never anywhere called the husband of Hera, and the Dodona oracle was throughout its long history served by priestesses. The oracle was an incubation oracle, a dream oracle, the kind of oracle typically associated with a goddess cult. (There is a tale about Zeus and this oracle that, if we didn't know better, we might rather have assigned to Hermes: it is said that Zeus first approached the nymph Io by whispering seductively to her in her dreams. When her father inquired of the oracle at Dodona what such dreams might mean, he was told to let his daughter go to the god.)

Except at Dodona, Dione pretty much disappears from view (though she appears in Homer as the mother of Aphrodite). Zeus goes on to make his way further into Greece, picking up mothers, sisters, wives, mistresses, daughters wherever he goes. All the earlier goddesses are in one role or another adopted into his family, though some come to be seen as nymphs, minor deities, rather than full-blown goddesses, and some like Helen or Clytemnestra are reduced to human status, viewed as mortal daughters of their divine father.

The Zeus religion also comes to absorb that of the already present male gods, whether they had begun as part of the old goddess religion or had arrived in Greece with earlier invaders. We have already seen throughout this book that as their rites are assimilated into the pan-Greek religious system, these gods become fathers, brothers, or sons to Zeus. In some cases, however, Zeus absorbs indigenous gods more thoroughly — though never as literally as he absorbed the goddess Metis, whom he swallowed! Their names are added to his as epithets. Zeus is not only Olympian Zeus, he is also Zeus Trophonios, Zeus the nourisher, a Zeus who has incorporated the cult of an ancient chthonic god associated with an oracular dream cult. He is Zeus Meilichios, Zeus the gentle; this Zeus has taken over the traditions associated with a snakegod whose nightly rituals provide expiation for kin murder. Zeus Meilichios represents the euphemistic side of a chthonic god who is also spoken of as Zeus Maimaktes, Zeus eager for blood. In Arcadia Zeus absorbs the cult of a native god of expiation associated with the fertilizing rain who was worshiped with human sacrifice.

The most important of these amalgamations took place in Crete where Zeus was identified with a native god associated with a wild, ecstatic, mystic cult. This Zeus is so different from the Olympian Zeus that he is often referred to as the "Cretan Zeus," and yet he *is* Zeus. Much of what we know of this cult and its myth may sound more like Dionysos than Zeus to us, but the arriving Hellenes identified this local god with their Zeus. And much that we think of as our Zeus, especially many of the traditions associated with his childhood, would disappear if we tried to extract the Cretan elements. These Cretan elements include the story of Cronos swallowing Zeus's older siblings and of Zeus being rescued from suffering the same fate when his mother hides him at birth; the focus on the protection offered the newborn god by the earth goddess, his grandmother Gaia; the tale of the Kuretes' wild and noisy dancing designed to conceal the infant's hiding place; the tradition of his being suckled by a goat or sow and fed by bees while concealed in a Cretan cave. According to this cycle of myths Zeus is the youngest child of Rhea and Cronos and the only one never swallowed by the father. Zeus is preeminently a *child,* the child of the mother. And in Crete Zeus not only has a childhood; he has a death, a grave.

Olympian Zeus, Homer's Zeus, on the other hand, has no childhood. As Guthrie says, for Homer there could be no birth story, no childhood traditions associated with Zeus, for "it is

Zeus to be in charge."[5] For Homer, Zeus is "the father of gods and men," the father who is always already father and assured of forever staying father. But fatherhood was probably not an original element of the Zeus tradition; it became a part of what the experience of Zeus encompassed when the patriarchal family came into existence. Zeus was the name spontaneously given to the highest thing in that new context, for Zeus *is,* as Kerenyi reminds us, the immediately recognized superiority over all divine and nondivine beings.[6] His fatherhood continues to mean simply that hegemony, not fatherhood in the stereotypical patriarchal sense. Zeus fathers many children, divine and human, but he is never the typical father with a son who will succeed him. Hera remains always too powerful, too independent, to fit into the role of a patriarch's wife and so she cannot have a patriarch's children. (We've seen the truth of this in our examination of Hephaistos and Ares.) In the case of Leto's son, Apollo, Zeus is only the originally anonymous procreative father given a name.[7] Nor is Zeus an ancestor god like, for instance, Apollo and Poseidon. He is the father of all Greeks but not the eponymous forefather of any Greek tribe.

Though he undoubtedly begins as a nature god, as a god of the lightning bolt and the mountaintop, except as metaphor this aspect is of little importance to the Zeus of the post-Homeric Greeks. There are reminders of this aspect in myth; for example, when Semele begs Zeus to visit her in his true form he comes as the lightning bolt whose fire consumes her, and in his abduction of Ganymede Zeus takes on the form of an eagle. Zeus was never imagined as a cosmogonic creator; the world is always already there when he appears. His concern is with the sphere of human life, particularly with the ordering of the human community. He is a human male writ large.

But myth as well as cult reveals how much of his power this father of the gods owes to females. We have already noted how at birth he is rescued by his mother Rhea and her mother Gaia from being devoured by his paranoid father and then is raised by nymphs. But we should also recall how essential Metis's wise counsel and provision of the magic emetic is to Zeus's successful rescue of his father-swallowed siblings — and later albeit involuntarily, Metis gives him her wisdom as he swallows her! Nor would Zeus and his generation have won their battle against the male Titans had the female Titans, Rhea and Gaia, not come to the aid of the younger gods against their own brothers. Another female Titan, Themis, and her daughter Dike, both identified as goddesses of order in the natural world and in the human community, continue to fulfill their roles in the new world established by Zeus.

Zeus overthrows his father (as his father, Cronos, has earlier overthrown *his* father, Ouranos). He swallows Metis because of a prophecy that if she were to bear him a son, that son would eventually take Zeus's power as his own; the family history leads Zeus to take this threat seriously. Zeus decides not to marry the Nereid Thetis, when he learns that the same prophecy has been made with regard to her. These precautions assure that no son born to Zeus ever comes close to threatening his sovereignty.

But Zeus accepts his daughter, Athene, as a worthy heir, sees her as more like him than are any of his sons, and encourages her in her every endeavor. He is proud of her wisdom and courage, her prudence and her benevolent support of the heroes who win her favor. Anna Freud had a father like that and in her life I plainly see the gains and the losses.[8] I have a father like that and have known it mostly as a blessing, though I also see how my brother has suffered from being less "the favored son" than I.

Though Zeus has no son to whom he is as close as he is to Athene, I am struck that in the *Odyssey* we are given a scene of a reconciliation between a father and son that to my mind matches in beauty and power the description of the reunion between Demeter and Persephone in "The Hymn to Demeter." And this father-son reunion would not have happened without the active support of Athene. The scene begins with Odysseus addressing Telemakhos:

"I am that father whom your boyhood lacked
and suffered pain for lack of. I am he."
. . . .
. . . . . *then, throwing*
his arms around this marvel of a father
Telemakhos began to weep. Salt tears
rose from the wells of longing in both men,
and cries burst forth from both as keen and fluttering
as those of the great taloned hawk,
whose nestlings farmers take before they fly.
So helplessly they cried, pouring out tears,
and might have gone on weeping so till sundown.[9]

Extrapolating from her own bond with Zeus, Athene can imagine a tenderness between fathers and sons that her own father could never show his male children.

Zeus is somehow comfortable with a dependence on mothers and daughters, at ease in the role of son of one female and father to another. He seems less at ease in the role of husband, consort, lover — as though he doesn't know which of these he is supposed to be, as though relating to females of the same generation, of equal power, is too confusing.

Not that Zeus isn't involved with many women in these other roles. Indeed, he is represented as endowed with seemingly inexhaustible sexual potency. Someone has counted them up and calculated that Zeus had at least 115 mistresses![10] And the mythology is full of wonderful stories about the ruses and metamorphoses upon which Zeus relies to accomplish his rapes and seductions.

Zeus transforms himself and often his prey as well. The myths offer us powerful, troubling images of male lust overpowering female reluctance. In a poem sequence called "Arachne's Tapestry" (based on Ovid's account of the tales woven into the tapestry Arachne creates in her competition to determine whether she or Athene is the more gifted weaver) River Malcolm recreates some of these disturbing scenes:

I weave Asteria, already mother of the
goddess Hecate, Zeus in lust grasping
at my mature body as at a prize in a
contest, and I defy him and run,
call forth the full power of my long
Titan legs, hurl my own body into the
sea, since I'd sooner drown than suffer
his siege, but he furious with frustration
changes me into a quail, small soft
feathered quarry, now seized in his
eagle talons, now Zeus of the sky
holds open my fragile bird body to his
battering phallus. My bones snap and crack,
muscles and ligaments rip, feathers fly.
Panting Zeus bursts to the summit of desire
as, still and broken, I lie, my limp neck
dangling from his slowly relaxing grip,
until he drops my body into the sea.

. . . .

I weave Alcmene, hand trembling
as I part the smooth satins that
curtain my bed, to admit
Amphitryon, beloved husband,
who enters and lies with me in the
nakedness of our first night. I
relive this moment again and
again, the curtain opening, the
man like a god. How could I not
know the disguise? As I see the
light fade from my husband's hurt
eyes, as I gasp for life through labor
stretched seven days by Hera's rage,
as I live to see my halfgod grown son
go mad and murder his children —
again and again, the curtain opens:
how could I not know the god?

I weave Antiope, hypnotized by the
satyr disguise of Zeus, with nimble
little goat hooves that prance and
cavort, a lewd smile on his lips
as he fondles a wooden flute, as his
fingers dance on the flute, teasing a
melody forth to caress my entire
untouchable skin, especially to lick
and tickle my young and unopened
bud, while he, winking, promises
music wilder than this, if I will
allow him to play on my body. Too
dizzy to deny him, I yield my flesh
as the frenzied tune of his touch
stretches me open to ripples
of ever widening pleasure, until
I am left, pregnant with twins,
facing my father's wrath.[11]

Not that it is always clear which are rapes and which seductions. Certainly Hera is always ready to see the other women
as all too willingly yielding to him; but sometimes the women
themselves seem unsure. Often there is a sequence of reluctance followed by a momentary rush of unexpected pleasure
and then, after the god has gone, regret:

I weave Danaë, locked in first
bloom in my underground prison,
bars so tight only air and rain can
squeeze through, my father crazy in
his need to keep me a virgin, somehow
to defeat the Delphic oracle, not
to die at the hands of my son.
When Zeus does come as gold rain,
I spread open my arms and hands,
loose my bodice, lift my skirt,
allow raindrops to dance on my

ankles and feet — this is the moment
of which the Oracle spoke: for this
god's pleasure, and mine, my father
will die. I lift my face to the rain,
feel the god stream down my eyelids,
cheeks, tongue, feel the god flow
down my throat, breast, belly, thigh.
I writhe on wet earth, my knees shake,
my thirsting fingers spread open
the flower of my girlhood to the
thrust and the pounding of rain,
my hips lift and stretch to receive,
in roaring cascade, the god's need.
I say let my father die.

I weave Aegina, seemingly unharmed
when the flame of the god licks my
body to hot coals, when the fire of
the god entwines my skin so tightly
I need never again feel cold or alone.
I go willingly with him to Oenone island,
and willingly bear him a child. But where
is Zeus, my burning god of a lover,
when his pleasure is done, and Hera
slips snake poison into the water,
leaving my son with no mother.[12]

One of the best known of these metamorphoses is that of Zeus coming to Leda (the mother of Helen and Clytemnestra and the Dioscuri) in the form of a swan:

I weave Leda, soon to be mother of Helen,
thrown to the ground by Zeus the swan,
deafened by the thunder of his wings,
blinded by the snake lightning of his neck,
my arms struck and bruised by his beak until
I can't fight or speak, until I dissolve. Finned

feet stroke and part me like water, white
plumage blazes, as swan-Zeus the
conqueror glides into my harbor, sowing
the seed of the fire that will consume Troy. [13]

This, again, is a woman poet's way of imagining their embrace. But Yeats's "Leda and the Swan" also envisions the god's entrance as brute mastery:

A sudden blow; the great wings beating still
Above the staggering girl, her thighs caressed
By the dark webs, her nape caught in his bill,
He holds her helpless breast upon his breast.

How can these terrified vague fingers push
The feathered glory from her loosening thighs?
And how can body, laid in that white rush,
But feel the strange heart beating where it lies? [14]

Whereas Rilke, imagining the scene from the god's perspective rather than the woman's, understands it differently:

When the god in his great need crossed inside,
he was shocked almost to find the swan so beau-
tiful;
he slipped himself inside it all confused.

. . . .

. . . . . *And the opened woman*
saw at once who was coming in the swan
and understood: he asked one *thing*

which she, confused in her resistance,
no longer could hold back. The god came down,

. . . .

released himself into the one he loved.
Then only — with what delight! — he felt his feath-
ers
and grew truly swan within her womb. [15]

Underneath the surface in these accounts of Zeus over-powering a female, there is often another more hidden story in which she plays the dominant role, for many of these tales are at least at one level mythological versions of the amalga-mation of cults, the amalgamation of an aboriginal goddess cult into the Zeus-dominated later religion.

Thus, for example, there is the tale of Zeus's "rape" of beautiful young Europa. The story begins with Zeus trans-forming himself into a white bull and joining a herd of cattle that Hermes had led to the seashore where Europa and some companions were playing. Entranced by the gentle crocus-munching bull, Europa climbed on his back. The bull entered the sea with the girl still astride and swam to Crete. There they made love under a plane tree which, so the story goes, never thereafter lost its leaves. The god gave Europa three gifts to protect her from harm and she bore him three sons, Minos, Rhadamanthys, and Sarpedon.

At one level, of course, as Malcolm perceives this is an account of a rape:

> *I weave Europa, girlchild, wide-eyed*
> *and curious to stroke the flank of the*
> *bull, his body white as poured milk,*
> *spring cloud, fresh snow sleeping*
> *on pine bough, pale glow of*
> *expectant moon, who grazes not*
> *as other bulls do on tough grass,*
> *but reclines and with great lips*
> *and long tongue delicately sips and*
> *caresses deep purple, glistening*
> *gold petals of flowers, so gentle*
> *I giggle and hug him, climb the smooth*
> *curve of his back, safe in knowing*
> *no one has ever wanted to hurt me*
> *until he leaps, sudden and huge, to*
> *the sea, the blade of his leap severing*
> *me from known shore, from my*

family, the cold wet splash of terror
on feet, legs, hands, arms — no longer
free, these puppet limbs that recoil
from drowning and cling to the god.[16]

At another level it represents the absorption of a matrilineal cult into Olympian religion. That Zeus takes the girl to Crete suggests the tale was originally associated with the Cretan Zeus and that the lovemaking of Zeus and Europa was once associated with a fertility ritual. The myth is very likely the reworking of an older tale in which a Cretan moon goddess triumphantly rides a bull, an animal long identified in Cretan worship as the goddess's consort. Thus the tale of an anthropomorphic god disguising himself as a bull may really represent a reversal of what happened in cult history: an originally theriomorphic deity becoming a humanlike male god. A story about the goddess riding her bull has become the story of a mortal woman being raped by the all-powerful god disguised as a bull.

Many of the stories reveal the tension between the patriarchal and the matriarchal perspective, the new god and the old goddess, men and women. The stories suggest that what is sought would be true lovemaking, but what happens is a power struggle that one or the other seems to win, but never definitively. We see this most dramatically in Zeus's relation to Hera. Their marriage *is* that struggle; it is not really about erotic passion or founding a family. The relationship is filled with tension and conflict, betrayal, recrimination, jealousy. There is also a tradition that through living out rather than evading this struggle they finally achieve a harmonious reconciliation. I recall Aeschylus's description of Zeus as the god "who has laid it down that wisdom comes alone through suffering."[17] Zeus's marriage to Hera, remember, is the one relationship that Zeus *stays* in. According to this tradition, convinced that he will never be the faithful husband she longs for, Hera leaves Zeus and returns to her Argive homeland where she bathes in a magic spring from which she emerges having recovered her virginity, her in-her-selfness. When she learns that Zeus is about to remarry, she can't resist going disguised to this wedding between Zeus and a woman whose identity he refuses to reveal. When at the climax of the ceremony the bride's veil is lifted, the spectators discover that she is nothing but a clumsily carved wood statue, that the event had been designed from beginning to end simply as a ruse to get Hera's attention. She laughs, he laughs, and they go off together.

We misunderstand Zeus if we see him only as a hypermasculine stud. For, although Dionysos is the only god who is ever referred to as "the womanly one," Zeus also has a "womanly" side. He swallows Metis and thus, we are told, absorbs her *metis,* her wisdom, and makes it his own. He gives birth to both Dionysos and Athene. He adopts the guise of a goddess, Artemis, when he makes love to the beautiful nymph, Callisto. We can read these myths as signifying Zeus's usurping the female role, as yet another act of male domination, or we can read them as suggesting a kind of fantasized transcendence of gender, as hinting at the importance of being able to live, at least imaginatively, from the other side.

How different in this respect, as in so many others, Zeus is from YHVH, a god so separated from the goddess, from mother, that he doesn't even have one. I love Nietzsche's image of the old gods and goddesses laughing themselves to death as they watch the young upstart Hebrew god strutting around claiming to be the only god![18] To be YHVH, YHVH has to be the only show in town. Though some claim he is a god who transcends gender differentiation, the masculine pronouns and epithets reveal a deeper truth. This god so intent on eradicating all reminders of mother-worship, so imbued with a dominating attitude toward nature, other peoples, and women is a very masculine god, in the most stereotypical sense of masculinity.

Whereas, as Farnell notes, it is striking that Zeus, originally the god of a warrior people, is so emphatically *not* a war god, nor a god who triumphs by virtue of physical superiority.[19]

Even in his battles against Cronos, and then in those against the Titans and the Giants, Zeus succeeds only by means of assistance received from the ancient goddesses. In the *Iliad* he stands aloof from the conflict. As Zeus Soter, Zeus the helper of men, his function is not so much to bring victory as to deliver his people from the perils of war. Zeus takes authority for the sake of peace and lawful order. Farnell also shows how the sculptural representations of Zeus, though they give him a well-muscled upper body to make manifest his divine power and energy, tend (especially in the later period) to highlight his deeply furrowed brow, to present him as more a god of reflection than of action.

And Zeus is also Zeus Chthonios, Zeus of the underworld, a Zeus who can be identified with Hades. To speak of him as "womanly," as in touch with his feminine side, seems to me to be but a preliminary and inadequate way of saying something that the image of the nether Zeus helps us say more clearly. Zeus is a god in touch with the *depths* of the psyche who also knows how to act in the upper world: For the Greeks both are aspects of his masculinity. Full honoring of this god moves us beyond any conventional understandings of "the masculine" or "the feminine."

The Greeks understood Zeus as a god secure in rule, a god who maintains order without suppressing diversity, vitality, life. It is true that Zeus was at one time plotted against by Hera, Athene, and Poseidon, but that was long ago and even then his power was never seriously threatened. He is the first in the line of chief deities who isn't overthrown (as Gaia, Ouranos, and Cronos all had been), because he embodies a different kind of order. Although some have seen in the Greek view of Zeus as a god involved with every aspect of life the beginnings of a move toward a monotheistic religion, I see Zeus as embodying Greek *polytheism,* an order that includes without suppressing difference. I like to remember that Zeus is among so much else Zeus Xenios, the god ready to honor the sanctity of the guest, the stranger, the alien. Scully suggests that precisely because Zeus is so open to all that appears, he is "above all else the god of things as they are," the god who brings us "the knowledge of things as they are" — and the acceptance that that is how it is.[20]

We noted above how Apollo is often called the most Greek of all the gods and how what he represents is the apparently victorious struggle of the new gods over the old, order over chaos, human civilization over the natural world. But, as Scully says so beautifully, by the early fifth century B.C.E. the Greeks seem to have been able to imagine a more integral, harmonious balancing between the old and the new, the natural and the human world, a balancing that Zeus embodies.

> Zeus was the true successor of the old goddess, from whom, in myth, he had usurped power through marriage and with a certain violence and cunning, as he had also usurped it from his father Kronos. His most important sanctuaries, therefore, were placed in those kinds of sites which had been most sacred to the goddess. . . . They are not necessarily the sites of the greatest violence and drama — except for the drama of the sky — as many of Apollo's sites are. Their meaning is not struggle but dominion.[21]

Scully helps us see the complex interrelationships among the temples at Olympia as expressing

> a mature reconciliation between the rebellious son and the necessarily overthrown father; between the new god and the goddess whom he had equally overthrown; between the brother Zeus and the sister Hera, husband and wife, whose life together had been, in myth since Homer, a continual and bitter strike. In the calm of the relationship may be felt, therefore, [a] reconciliation between men and nature, men and women, and between the old gods and the new.[22]

This is the Zeus I know, the Zeus who represents what Jung called the Self, a god who encompasses all the variety, the tension, the conflict, the successes and failures, the wounds and the gifts, that are part of life as we humans experience it, a god who is *there* in the rare moments of conciliation *and* in all the moments of contention. Zeus, the god of things as they are. How can we help but honor him?

And yet, and yet... though this may be Zeus as Athene knows him, Zeus as I from time to time experience him, this will not do as an adequate representation of the primary ways in which Zeus enters into the consciousness of women.

Perhaps, as Scully imagines, Greek temple architecture does suggest a view of Zeus as a god who represents a reconciliation of the matristic and the patriarchal and of women and men. But surely the myths do not. And though we may go back behind the myths and discover through them remnants of more ancient traditions and hints of subversive subtexts, the myths themselves in their best-known versions are inextricably interwoven with the patriarchal structures of the classical Greek world and have in the intervening centuries undeniably helped shape and undergird the patriarchal structures of our world.

I believe it is important for us women to find in Zeus more than the rapist, to see him as representing a much more complex "masculinity" – but it is important also that we not forget that he is a rapist, that he was honored as the dominant deity in a society that radically suppressed women, and that one important way of understanding his "female" side is to see him as a male god who not only overwhelmed women but also usurped their female energies and made them his own.

Zeus's rapes were so often seductions; his intrusions were so often experienced as yielding intense though fleeting pleasure. Only afterward did the women recognize how alien was this power to which they had succumbed. Only afterward did they recognize that he had used them for his pleasure and then abandoned them. I recognize how easily Zeus seduces me, or rather how the Zeus energy in me too often leads me to adopt a male view that is not really my own, to be tricked once again into thinking that a male paradigm can provide me with access to my own deepest truths. Zeus, my Zeus, may, indeed, serve as a Self image for men; he cannot serve as such for me.

The Zeus I have been describing is in a sense a fantasy — a fantasy created out of bits and pieces of the ancient traditions about Zeus woven together in a way that the Greeks never had. But the Greek gods were, as we noted in chapter 1, always still in process. And what I see the Greek Zeus as helping us proceed toward is a postpatriarchal image of male wholeness, a woman's view of what men might be like. It is my fantasy not about myself, but about men. This "postpatriarchal" Zeus is a Zeus aware of his dependence on the prepatriarchal world, the world of the goddesses, a Zeus aware of how much of his power he owes to females, a Zeus not so fearful of powerful women that he needs to win dominion over them, a Zeus who has come to acknowledge and value those vulnerable and nurturing and harmonizing sides of himself that represent energies conventionally regarded as "feminine."

This Zeus is the counterplayer for whom I yearn, a counterplayer whom I have glimpsed as a possibility through some of the men I have most loved, including the one to whom this book is dedicated. For I believe that we women cannot really move toward living as postpatriarchal women unless men become postpatriarchal men. If they don't, we will at best find ourselves in a *contra*patriarchal world, not truly a *post*patriarchal one.

But Zeus also reminds me that what I hope toward is, indeed, the creation of a postpatriarchal humanity, not a return to a prepatriarchal one. We may be able to go on; we cannot go back. Thus although I see Zeus as helping us to imagine a postpatriarchal form of male energy, I also believe it is important for us to keep in view his connection to patriarchal perspectives. Zeus helps us to move forward precisely by reminding us, all of us, men as well as women, of the persistence of that which we must strive against.

Zeus, as we noted at the beginning of this chapter, represents divine energy as event, as overwhelming power. There is that kind of divine power. But we women also know divine energy that is more intimate, that is not so *other*, that flows through our veins rather than entering us from outside. Rightly to honor the gods requires of us that we remember also the homage due the goddesses. Zeus cannot be a Self image for women, nor, I believe, can any of the gods. The gods enter us in important ways – they *are* in our midst. We need to acknowledge them, welcome them – and be wary of them.

Notes

Chapter 1: Attending to the Gods

1. Philip Zabriskie, "Goddesses in our Midst," *Quadrant,* Fall 1974.
2. Robert Bly, *Iron John* (Reading, Mass.: Addison-Wesley, 1990), 235, 236.
3. For a more elaborated discussion of my perspective on gender and essentialism, see my *Women's Mysteries* (New York: Crossroad, 1992), especially chaps. 2 and 3.
4. See William Doty, *Myths of Masculinity* (New York: Crossroad, forthcoming).
5. Walter F. Otto, *The Homeric Gods* (Boston: Beacon Press, 1964), 160-61.
6. See my *The Goddess: Mythological Images of the Feminine* (New York: Crossroad, 1981), 238-39.
7. See my *Journey through Menopause* (New York: Crossroad, 1987), 45-47.
8. H.D., *Collected Poems 1912-1944* (New York: New Directions, 1983), 124.
9. Jean-Pierre Vernant, *Mortals and Immortals* (Princeton: Princeton University Press, 1991), 7.
10. See James Hillman, "The Great Mother, Her Son, Her Hero, and the Puer," in Patricia Berry, ed., *Fathers and Mothers* (Zurich: Spring Publications, 1973), 75-127.
11. See Demaris Wehr, "Uses and Abuses of Jung's Psychology of Women: Animus," *Anima* 12, no. 1 (Fall 1985): 13-23.
12. Karl Kerenyi, *Hermes: Guide of Souls* (Zurich: Spring Publications, 1976), 55.
13. Rainer Maria Rilke, *Samtliche Werke II* (Wiesbaden: Insel Verlag, 1956), 468.
14. Martin P. Nilsson, *The Mycenaean Origin of Greek Mythology* (Berkeley, Calif.: University of California Press, 1972), 222.
15. Carl Kerenyi, *Zeus and Hera* (Princeton: Princeton University Press, 1975), 39.
16. Vernant, *Mortals,* 271-73.
17. Lewis Richard Farnell, *The Cults of the Greek States* (Chicago: Aegean Press, 1971), 5:86, 87.

18. Vernant, *Mortals*, 287.
19. Friedrich Nietzsche, *The Birth of Tragedy* (New York: Doubleday Anchor, 1956), 30.
20. Kerenyi, *Hermes*, 1.
21. See Merlin Stone, *When God Was a Woman* (New York: Dial Press, 1976); Charlene Spretnak, *The Lost Goddesses of Early Greece* (Boston: Beacon Press, 1981).
22. Walter Burkert, *Greek Religion* (Cambridge, Mass.: Harvard University Press, 1985), 218.
23. Rafael Lopez-Pedraza, *Hermes and His Children* (Zurich: Spring Publications, 1977), 2.
24. Burkert, *Greek Religion*, 218.
25. Farnell, *Cults*, 1:30.
26. See my *Women's Mysteries* (New York: Crossroad, 1992), chap. 6.
27. Nilsson, *Mycenaean Origin*, 221-25.
28. Jane Ellen Harrison, *Prolegomena to the Study of Greek Religion* (New York: Meridian Books, 1957), 325, 332, 333, 17, 347, 338.
29. Vincent Scully, *The Earth, the Temple, and the Gods* (New Haven: Yale University Press, 1979), 27, 37-39, 26.
30. Scully, *The Earth*, 22.
31. Scully, *The Earth*, 42; see my chapter on Zeus at the end of this volume.
32. Scully, *The Earth*, 1, 3, 2.
33. Jean-Pierre Vernant, *Mortals*, 277.

Chapter 2: Hades and Cronos

1. For a fuller account of this dream see my *The Goddess*, chap. 1.
2. Indeed, I have gathered together some of the recent feminist retellings and interpretations of the myth in an anthology (to be published by Shambhala in late 1993), which makes visible the many perspectives constitutive of contemporary feminism.
3. George E. Mylonas, *Eleusis and the Eleusinian Mysteries* (Princeton: Princeton University Press, 1974), 199, 102; Lewis Richard Farnell, *The Cults of the Greek States* (Chicago: Aegean Press, 1971), 3:225, 257-58.
4. See my "Coming Home to Hestia," *Journey through Menopause* (New York: Crossroad, 1987), chap. 4.
5. Carl Kerenyi, *The Gods of the Greeks* (London: Thames and Hudson, 1979), 93.

6. Farnell, *Cults*, 1:110.

7. H. S. Versnel. "Greek Myth and Ritual: The Case of Kronos," in Jan Bremmer, ed., *Interpretations of Greek Mythology* (Totowa, N.J.: Barnes & Noble, 1986), 121-52.

8. Versnel, "Kronos," 143.

9. Versnel, "Kronos," 144, 146.

10. From a selection included in Burton Feldman and Robert D. Richardson, *The Rise of Modern Mythology 1680-1860* (Bloomington: Indiana University Press, 1972), 347.

11. Farnell, *Cults,* 3:287.

12. Kerenyi, *Gods,* 230.

13. Farnell, *Cults*, 3:285.

14. Walter Burkert, *Greek Religion* (Cambridge, Mass.: Harvard University Press, 1985), 297.

15. Kerenyi, *Gods,* 246.

16. Carl Kerenyi, *Dionysos: Archetypal Image of Indestructible Life* (Princeton: Princeton University Press, 1976), 35, 140.

17. Mylonas, *Eleusis,* 213, 214, 276, 309.

18. Veronique M. Foti, "Hades and Dionysos, *Spring 1983,* 126-28.

19. Burkert, *Greek Religion,* 128.

Chapter 3: Hermes

1. For earlier reflections on this experience, see *The Goddess: Mythological Images of the Feminine* (New York: Crossroad, 1981), 46-47, 241.

2. Lewis Richard Farnell, *The Cults of the Greek States* (Chicago: Aegean Press, 1971), 5:14.

3. Stephen Mitchell, trans., *The Selected Poetry of Rainer Maria Rilke* (New York: Random House, 1982), 51-53.

4. Although the Pythagoreans may have adopted Hermes as a guardian of souls; see Farnell, *Cults*, 5:15.

5. Charles Boer, *The Homeric Hymns* (Chicago: Swallow Press, 1970), 39-40, 60-61.

6. Kerenyi, *Hermes: Guide of Souls* (Zurich: Spring Publications, 1976), 62.

7. Kerenyi, *Hermes,* 17, 18, 24.

8. Walter F. Otto, *The Homeric Gods* (Boston: Beacon Press, 1964), 108.

9. Walter Burkert, *Greek Religion* (Cambridge, Mass.: Harvard University Press, 1985), 156.

10. Kerenyi, *Hermes,* 84.
11. Otto, *Homeric Gods,* 117.
12. Farnell, *Cults,* 5:24.
13. Kerenyi, *Hermes,* 84.
14. Kerenyi, *Hermes,* 71, 72, 75.
15. Kerenyi, *Hermes,* 45.
16. Kerenyi, *Hermes,* 51.
17. Rafael Lopez-Pedraza, *Hermes and His Children* (Zurich: Spring Publications, 1977), 4, 13.
18. Kerenyi, *Hermes,* 64.
19. Kerenyi, *Hermes,* 62.
20. Lopez-Pedraza, *Hermes,* 63.
21. See Lopez-Pedraza, *Hermes,* 95.
22. See Donald F. Nelson, *Portrait of the Artist as Hermes: A Study of Myth and Psychology in Thomas Mann's Felix Krull* (Chapel Hill: University of North Carolina Press, 1971).
23. H.D., *Collected Poems 1912-1944* (New York: New Directions, 1983), 37-39.
24. Janice S. Robinson, *H.D.: The Life and Work of an American Poet* (Boston: Houghton Mifflin, 1982), 34-36.
25. Robinson, *H.D.,* 71.
26. H.D., *Tribute to Freud* (New York: McGraw-Hill, 1974), 75.
27. H.D., *Tribute,* 76.
28. H.D., *Tribute,* 101-3.
29. Susan Stanford Friedman, *Psyche Reborn: The Emergence of H.D.* (Bloomington: Indiana University Press, 1981), 207, 212, 249, 220.
30. Ginette Paris, *Pagan Grace* (Dallas: Spring Publications, 1990), 85, 87.
31. See my *Goddess,* chap. 5.
32. Kerenyi, *Gods,* 171, 2.
33. Lopez-Pedraza, *Hermes,* 3.
34. Otto, *Homeric Gods,* 108, 120.
35. Kerenyi, *Hermes,* 91.
36. Otto, *Homeric Gods,* 115, 124.

Chapter 4: Dionysos

1. Walter F. Otto, *The Homeric Gods* (Boston: Beacon Press, 1964), 139.
2. Walter Burkert, *Greek Religion* (Cambridge, Mass.: Harvard University Press, 1985), 201-2.

3. Carl Kerenyi, *Dionysos: Archetypal Image of Indestructible Life* (Princeton: Princeton University Press, 1976), 119.

4. Jane Ellen Harrison, *Prolegomena to the Study of Greek Religion* (New York: Meridian Books, 1957), 378.

5. Harrison, *Prolegomena,* 404.

6. Harrison, *Prolegomena,* 402.

7. See my *Myths and Mysteries of Same-Sex Love* (New York: Continuum, 1989), 161-64.

8. Carl Kerenyi, *Zeus and Hera: Archetypal Image of Father, Husband, and Wife* (Princeton: Princeton University Press, 1975), 276.

9. Kerenyi, *Zeus,* 282.

10. Lewis Richard Farnell, *The Cults of the Greek States* (Chicago: Aegean Press, 1971), 5:119.

11. W. K. C. Guthrie, *The Greeks and Their Gods* (Boston: Beacon, 1955), 148.

12. At least according to the dominant tradition, which emphasizes his fidelity to Ariadne; there are, however, traditions according to which he fathered Althaea's daughter Deineira (who later married Herakles) and Aaraethyrea's son Phlias. See Edward Tripp, *Crowell's Handbook of Classical Mythology* (New York: Thomas Y. Crowell Company, 1970), 209.

13. H.D., *Collected Poems 1912-1944* (New York: New Directions, 1983), 45-46.

14. Harrison, *Prolegomena*, 364.

15. Kerenyi, *Dionysos,* 221, 124.

16. Harrison, *Prolegomena*, 411, 425.

17. Martin P. Nilsson, *A History of Greek Religion* (New York: Norton, 1964), 206.

18. Harrison, *Prolegomena,* 436.

19. Kerenyi, *Dionysos*, 241.

20. Harrison, *Prolegomena*, 444.

21. Farnell, *Cults,* 5:120.

22. Kerenyi, *Zeus,* 179, 201.

23. Kerenyi, *Dionysos*, 350.

24. Harrison, *Prolegomena*, 453.

25. Mylonas, *Eleusis*, 213, 214, 276, 309.

26. Harrison, *Prolegomena*, 150.

27. Harrison, *Prolegomena*, 363.

28. Robert Eisner, *The Road to Daulis* (Syracuse: Syracuse University Press, 1987), 120.

29. Harrison, *Prolegomena*, 391.

30. Farnell, *Cults,* 5:113, 114.

Chapter 5: Apollo

1. Carl Kerenyi, *Dionysos: Archetypal Image of Indestructible Life* (Princeton: Princeton University Press, 1976), xxiv.

2. See William Doty, *Myths of Masculinity* (New York: Crossroad, forthcoming), chap. 8; James Hillman, *The Myth of Analysis* (Evanston: Northwestern University Press, 1972), 266–70.

3. Walter F. Otto, *Dionysus: Myth and Cult* (Bloomington: Indiana University Press, 1965), 78.

4. Lewis Richard Farnell, *The Cults of the Greek States* (Chicago: Aegean Press, 1971), 4:267.

5. See Bernard Sargent, *Homosexuality in Greek Myth* (Boston: Beacon, 1986), 81–102.

6. Robert Eisner, *The Road to Daulis* (Syracuse: Syracuse University Press, 1987), 141.

7. Otto, *Dionysus*, 78.

8. Farnell, *Cults*, 4:265.

9. Farnell, *Cults*, 4:173.

10. Farnell, *Cults*, 4:113–15.

11. Alexander Gelley, trans., *Mythology and Humanism: The Correspondence of Thomas Mann and Karl Kerenyi* (Ithaca: Cornell University Press, 1975), 33.

12. W. K. C. Guthrie, *The Greeks and Their Gods* (Boston: Beacon, 1955), 203.

13. Martin P. Nilsson, *A History of Greek Religion* (New York: Norton, 1964), 156.

14. Otto, *Dionysus*, 65.

15. Farnell, *Cults*, 4:305–6.

16. Farnell, *Cults*, 4:299.

17. See my "Only the Wounded Healer Heals: The Testimony of Greek Mythology," *Soundings* 73, no. 4 (Winter 1990): 551–74.

18. Farnell, *Cults*, 4:282.

19. Jane Ellen Harrison, *Prolegomena to the Study of Greek Religion* (New York: Meridian Books, 1957), 103–4.

20. Farnell, *Cults*, 4:275.

21. Farnell, *Cults*, 4:284.

22. Philip Slater, *The Glory of Hera* (Boston: Beacon, 1971), 160–61.

23. Vincent Scully, *The Earth, the Temple, and the Gods* (New Haven: Yale University Press, 1979), 129–30.

24. See my *Women's Mysteries*, chap. 2.

25. Scully, *The Earth*, 100, 104, 105, 107.

26. May Sarton, *Collected Poems 1930–1973* (New York: Norton, 1974), 258–59.

27. Eisner, *Daulis,* 151.
28. H.D., "Evadne" (New York: New Directions, 1983), 132.
29. Harrison, *Prolegomena,* 394.
30. Harrison, *Prolegomena,* 394.
31. Erwin Rohde, *Psyche: The Cult of Souls and Belief in Immortality among the Greeks* (New York: Harper, 1966), 1:150-61.
32. Farnell, *Cults,* 4:192.
33. See Guilia Sasso, *Greek Virginity* (Cambridge, Mass.: Harvard University Press, 1990), chap. 5.
34. H.D. "At Piraeus," *Collected Poems,* 177, 179.
35. H.D. "Delphi," *Collected Poems,* 401.
36. Farnell, *Cults,* 4:250.
37. Farnell, *Cults,* 4:251.
38. Farnell, *Cults,* 4:152.
39. Farnell, *Cults,* 4:258.
40. Farnell, *Cults,* 4:203.
41. Guthrie, *The Greeks,* 189.
42. Scully, *The Earth,* 114.

Chapter 6: Hephaistos and Ares

1. Lewis Richard Farnell, *The Cults of the Greek States* (Chicago: Aegean Press, 1971), 5:375.
2. See Gerda Lerner, *The Creation of Patriarchy* (New York: Oxford University Press, 1986), esp. chap. 2.
3. Charles Boer, trans., *The Homeric Hymns* (Dallas: Spring Publications, 1970), 86.
4. Pierre Grimal, *The Dictionary of Classical Mythology* (New York: Basil Blackwell, 1987), 115.
5. Philip Morton, "Revisioning Hephaistos," 4, unpublished paper, cited with permission.
6. Charles Seltman, *The Twelve Olympians* (New York: Crowell, 1960), 92.
7. Murray Stein, "Hephaistos: A Pattern of Introversion," in James Hillman, ed., *Facing the Gods* (Irving, Tex.: Spring Publications, 1980), 67.
8. Farnell, *Cults,* 5:375.
9. Morton, "Revisioning," 11.
10. C. G. Jung, *Collected Works* (Princeton: Princeton University Press, 1953-79), vol. 5, esp. part 2, chap. 5.
11. Stein, "Hephaistos," 71.

12. Stein, "Hephaistos," 71.

13. See my *The Goddess: Mythological Images of the Feminine* (New York: Crossroad, 1981), chap. 4.

14. Richmond Lattimore, trans., *The Iliad of Homer* (Chicago: University of Chicago Press, 1951), bk. 5:831, p. 150.

15. *Iliad*, bk. 5:890, 897-98, p. 152.

16. *Oedipus Rex*, line 215.

17. Jane Ellen Harrison, *Prolegomena to the Study of Greek Religion* (New York: Meridian Books, 1957), 377.

18. Jean Bolen, *Gods in Every Man* (San Francisco: Harper & Row, 1989), 199.

19. See Robert Bly, *Iron John* (Reading, Mass.: Addison-Wesley, 1990).

20. Farnell, *Cults*, 5:405.

21. Seltman, *Olympians*, 102.

Chapter 7: Poseidon

1. See "Coming Home to Hestia" in my *Journey through Menopause* (New York: Crossroad, 1987).

2. Vincent Scully, *The Earth, the Temple, and the Gods* (New Haven: Yale University Press, 1979), 164.

3. Carl Kerenyi, *Zeus and Hera* (Princeton: Princeton University Press, 1975), 64, 65.

4. Walter F. Otto, *The Homeric Gods* (Boston: Beacon Press, 1964), 27.

5. Lewis Richard Farnell, *The Cults of the Greek States* (Chicago: Aegean Press, 1971), 4:1.

6. Edward Tripp, *Crowell's Handbook of Classical Mythology* (New York: Thomas Y. Crowell Company, 1970), 493.

7. Farnell, *Cults*, 4:45.

8. Scully, *The Earth*, 156.

9. Scully, *The Earth*, 157.

10. Tripp, *Handbook*, 62.

11. See my *Myths and Mysteries of Same-Sex Love* (New York: Continuum, 1989), 165-66.

Chapter 8: Zeus

1. Carl Kerenyi, *Zeus and Hera* (Princeton: Princeton University Press, 1975), 11.
2. Kerenyi, *Zeus,* iv, 13, 14, 18.
3. Kerenyi, *Zeus,* 5.
4. H.D., "Dodona," *Collected Poems 1912-1944* (New York: New Directions, 1983), 407, slightly rearranged.
5. W. K. C. Guthrie, *The Greeks and Their Gods* (Boston: Beacon, 1955), 40.
6. Kerenyi, *Zeus,* 46, 47, 49.
7. Kerenyi, *Zeus,* 45.
8. See Elisabeth Young-Bruehl, *Anna Freud* (New York: Summit, 1988).
9. Robert Fitzgerald, trans., *The Odyssey of Homer* (Garden City, N.Y.: Doubleday Anchor, 1963), bk. 16, lines 188-89, 215-20, 295, 296.
10. Walter Burkert, *Greek Religion* (Cambridge, Mass.: Harvard University Press, 1985), 128.
11. River Malcolm, "Arachne's Tapestry," *No Goddess Dances to a Mortal Tune* (Del Mar, Calif.: self-published, 1992), 25-27.
12. Malcolm, "Arachne's Tapestry," 27-28.
13. Malcolm, "Arachne's Tapestry," 26.
14. W. B. Yeats, "Leda and the Sawn," *Collected Poems* (New York, Macmillan, 1967), 211-12.
15. Edward Snow, trans., "Leda," *Rainer Maria Rilke: New Poems [1908]: The Other Part* (San Francisco: North Point Press, 1987), 7.
16. Malcolm, "Arachne's Tapestry," 24-25.
17. Aeschylus, *Agamemnon,* lines 177-78.
18. Friedrich Nietzsche, *Thus Spake Zarathustra* in *The Portable Nietzsche,* ed. and trans. Walter Kaufmann (Princeton: Princeton University Press, 1954), 294.
19. Lewis Richard Farnell, *The Cults of the Greek States,* 1:59.
20. Vincent Scully, *The Earth, the Temple, and the Gods* (New Haven: Yale University Press, 1979), 133.
21. Scully, *The Earth,* 133.
22. Scully, *The Earth,* 151.

Index